BASIS FOR BUSINESS

PHRASEBOOK

B2

BASIS FOR BUSINESS B2 Phrasebook

Im Auftrag des Verlages erarbeitet von	Zsuzsa Parádi
Redaktionelle Mitarbeit	Eva Schmidt
Redaktion	Anna Batrla
Projektleitung	Murdo MacPhail
Gesamtgestaltung und technische Umsetzung	eScriptum GmbH & Co KG, Berlin
Umschlagfoto	Shutterstock / Yuri Arcurs

www.cornelsen.de

1. Auflage, 3. Druck 2015

Alle Drucke dieser Auflage sind inhaltlich unverändert und können im Unterricht nebeneinander verwendet werden.

Druck: Firmengruppe APPL, aprinta Druck, Wemding

ISBN 978-3-06-521008-9

PEFC zertifiziert

Dieses Produkt stammt aus nachhaltig bewirtschafteten Wäldern und kontrollierten Quellen

PEFC/04-32-0928   www.pefc.de

Einleitung

Im **BASIS FOR BUSINESS B2 Phrasebook** können Sie die Wörter, die im Kursbuch vorkommen, in mehreren Verzeichnissen nachschlagen.

In der chronologischen Wortliste sind für jede englische Vokabel die deutsche Übersetzung sowie die Aussprache der Vokabel in phonetischer Umschrift angegeben.

Diese Wortliste enthält darüber hinaus Kästen, in denen wichtige Redewendungen thematisch für Sie zusammengefasst sind. So sehen Sie auf einen Blick, mit welchen sprachlichen Mitteln Sie sich in bestimmten geschäftlichen Situationen am besten ausdrücken können.

Die Reihenfolge der Wörter in der chronologischen Liste entspricht der Reihenfolge ihres Auftretens in den einzelnen Units. Als Orientierungshilfe sind die Wörter den einzelnen Teilen einer Unit *(Part A, Part B, Part C, Grammar summary, Extra practice)* bzw. den Hörtexten zugeordnet. Die Information zur Fundstelle steht auch am jeweiligen Seitenende. Die *Exercise*-Nummern links neben den Wörtern helfen Ihnen dabei, das entsprechende Wort im Kursbuch schnell zu finden.

Darüber hinaus bietet das **BASIS FOR BUSINESS B2 Phrasebook** ein alphabetisches Register (Englisch-Deutsch) zum schnellen Nachschlagen einzelner Begriffe sowie eine Liste zu Orten, Ländern und Nationalitäten.

Viel Spaß beim Lernen mir Ihrem **BASIS FOR BUSINESS B2 Phrasebook**!

Inhalt

Verwendete Abkürzungen

GS	Grammar summary	jmd	jemand
coll.	colloquial (umgangssprachlich)	jmdm	jemandem
sth	something	jmdn	jemanden
sb	somebody	jmds	jemandes
etw	etwas		

Verwendete Symbole

⏵ warm-up exercise

🔊" Hörtext

Hinweise zur Aussprache

ɑː wie in **a**sk [ɑːsk]

ʌ wie in n**u**mber ['nʌmbə]

æ wie in c**a**n [kæn]

e wie in **e**nter ['entə]

iː wie in h**e** [hiː]

i wie in happ**y** ['hæpi]

ɪ wie in s**i**t [sɪt]

ɜː wie in b**i**rthday ['bɜːθdeɪ]

ɒ wie in g**o**t [gɒt]

ɔː wie in f**ou**r [fɔː]

ʊ wie in b**oo**k [bʊk]

uː wie in f**oo**d [fuːd]

u wie in sit**u**ation [ˌsɪtʃu'eɪʃn]

ə wie in fath**er** ['fɑːðə]

aɪ wie in fl**igh**t ['flaɪt]

aʊ wie in **ou**t [aʊt]

eɪ wie in d**a**te [deɪt]

ɔɪ wie in b**oy** [bɔɪ]

ɪə wie in h**ear** [hɪə]

eə wie in h**air** [heə]

əʊ wie in ph**o**ne [fəʊn]

Welcome!

1	Executive PA (= Executive Personal Assistant)	[ɪg͵zekjətɪv ͵piː 'eɪ]	Chefsekretär/in, persönliche/r Referent/in der Geschäftsführung
	VP (= vice-president)	[͵viː 'piː]	Vizepräsident/in
	Chief Information Officer (= CIO)	[͵tʃiːf ɪnfə͵meɪʃn 'ɒfɪsə]	Leiter/in der Abteilung Informationstechnologie
	distributer	[dɪ'strɪbjətə]	Vertreiber/in
	Customer technical support representative	[͵kʌstəmə teknɪkl sə͵pɔːt reprɪ'zentətɪv]	Beauftragte/r für die technische Kundenbetreuung
	automation	[͵ɔːtə'meɪʃn]	Automatisierung
1.2	to go along with sb	[gəʊ ə'lɒŋ wɪð]	jmdn begleiten
	business entertaining	[bɪznəs entə'teɪnɪŋ]	Geschäftsveranstaltungen
	to keep up	[͵kiːp 'ʌp]	mithalten
1.3	latest	['leɪtəst]	neueste/r/s
	to keep up to date	[kiːp ͵ʌp tə 'deɪt]	auf dem neuesten Stand halten
	while	[waɪl]	Weile
	to take a while	[teɪk ə 'waɪl]	eine Weile dauern
	to adjust	[ə'djʌst]	einstellen
	to get better at	[get 'betər ət]	besser werden in
1.4	conference call	['kɒnfərəns kɔːl]	Telefonkonferenz
2	to entertain	[͵entə'teɪn]	unterhalten, einladen
	manual	['mænjuəl]	Handbuch
4	pie	['paɪ]	Torte
	pie chart	['paɪ tʃɑːt]	Tortendiagramm
5	lean	[liːn]	schlank, verschlankt
	to explore	[ɪk'splɔː]	untersuchen, prüfen
	service	['sɜːvɪs]	Kundenbetreuung
	to review	[rɪ'vjuː]	durchsehen, prüfen
	treatment	['triːtmənt]	Behandlung
	water treatment plant	['wɔːtə triːtmənt plɑːnt]	Wasseraufbereitungsanlage, Kläranlage
	to brief	[briːf]	informieren, instruieren
6	secondment	[sɪ'kɒndmənt]	vorübergehende Versetzung
	to be on secondment	[͵bi ɒn sɪ'kɒndmənt]	vorübergehend versetzt sein

... is a medium sized manufacturer of ... that is based in ...	... ist ein ein mittelgroßer Hersteller von ... mit Sitz in ...
... is a leading provider of ... with head-quarters in ...	... ist ein führender Anbieter von ... mit Hauptsitz in ...
... is a leading player in the development of ...	... ist federführend bei der Entwicklung von ...
Our products are both future-oriented and environmentally friendly.	Unsere Produkte sind sowohl zukunfts-orientiert als auch umweltfreundlich.
We are committed to improving ... by ...	Wir haben uns der Verbesserung von/der ... mithilfe von ... verpflichtet.
We guarantee that our highly-qualified and flexible teams will ...	Wir garantieren, dass unsere hoch-qualifizierten und flexiblen Teams ...
I've been reading up on your company.	Ich habe mich über Ihr Unternehmen informiert.

1A, At a networking conference

try	[traɪ]	Versuch
Have a try!	[ˌhəv ə 'traɪ]	Versuch's mal!
decision-maker	[dɪ'sɪʒn meɪkə]	Entscheidungsträger/in

I have to negotiate a deal involving ...	Ich muss ein Geschäft verhandeln, bei dem es um ... geht.
I am exploring ways to make production methods more efficient.	Ich suche nach Wegen, um Produktions-methoden effizienter zu machen.
I hope to interest the board of ...	Ich hoffe, dass ich beim Vorstand von ... Interesse wecken kann.
I ask customers for feedback on ...	Ich frage Kunden nach ihrer Meinung zu ...

1	to strike up sth	[ˌstraɪk 'ʌp]	etw beginnen
	keynote	['kiːnəʊt]	Leitgedanke
	keynote speech	['kiːnəʊt spiːtʃ]	Eröffnungsrede
1.5	turbine	['tɜːbaɪn]	Turbine
	wind	[wɪnd]	Wind
	tubing	['tjuːbɪŋ]	Rohr, Schlauch
	wind turbine tower	['wɪnd tɜːbaɪn taʊə]	Windkraftrad
	development engineer	[dɪ'veləpmənt endʒɪ'nɪə]	Entwicklungsingenieur/in
	transportation	[ˌtrænspɔː'teɪʃn]	Transport
	later on	[leɪtər 'ɒn]	später

Excuse me. I don't believe we've met. I'm …	Entschuldigung. Ich glaube, wir kennen uns noch nicht. Ich bin …
I'd like to introduce you to someone.	Ich würde Sie gerne jemandem vorstellen.
Have you met …? He's also based in …	Haben Sie … kennengelernt? Er arbeitet auch in …
Pleased/Nice to meet you.	Freut mich, Sie kennenzulernen.
How are you doing / How are things with you?	Wie geht es Ihnen?
It was nice seeing you again / meeting you.	Es war schön, Sie wiederzusehen / Sie kennenzulernen.
Same here. Catch you later, maybe? / Let's catch up later.	Gleichfalls. Vielleicht sehen wir uns später noch?
Maybe we'll bump into each other later.	Vielleicht laufen wir uns später über den Weg.

4	recording	[rɪˈkɔːdɪŋ]	Aufzeichnung
5	pipe	[paɪp]	Rohr, Leitung
	reorganization	[riːˌɔːrɡənəˈzeɪʃn]	Umorganisation, Neuorganisation
1.6	to bump into sb	[bʌmp ˈɪntə]	jmdn zufällig treffen
	congratulations	[kənˌɡrætʃuˈleɪʃn]	Gratulation, Glückwunsch
	promotion	[prəˈməʊʃn]	Aufstieg, Beförderung
	central	[ˈsentrəl]	zentral
	nuisance	[ˈnjuːsns]	Ärger
	It drives me crazy!	[ɪt ˌdraɪvz mi ˈkreɪzi]	Das macht mich verrückt!
	initiative	[ɪˈnɪʃətɪv]	Initiative, Anstoß
6	to keep going	[kiːp ˈɡəʊɪŋ]	am Laufen halten
	intonation	[ɪntəˈneɪʃn]	Intonation, Sprachmelodie
	trade link	[ˈtreɪd lɪŋk]	Handelsverbindung

Would you excuse me for a moment? I've just spotted someone I need to talk to.	Würden Sie mich einen Moment entschuldigen? Ich habe gerade jemanden gesehen, den ich sprechen muss.
Are you happy with your progress in the market?	Sind Sie mit Ihrer Entwicklung auf dem Markt zufrieden?
Do you think there's a big market for …?	Denken Sie, es gibt einen großen Markt für …?

1B, Company facts

▶ hierarchical	[ˌhaɪəˈrɑːkɪkl]	hierarchisch
hybrid	[ˈhaɪbrɪd]	Mischung
matrix	[ˈmeɪtrɪks]	Gerüst, Netz, Matrix
procurement	[prəˈkjʊəmənt]	Beschaffung

1	mixture	['mɪkstʃə]	Mischung
	tall	[tɔːl]	hoch
	to turn	[tɜːn]	umdrehen
	beside	[bɪ'saɪd]	neben
	to get sb to do sth	[ˌget tə 'duː]	jmdn dazu bekommen, etwas zu tun
	amount	[ə'maʊnt]	Menge
	sort of (coll.)	['sɔːt əv]	irgendwie
	to go blank	[gəʊ 'blæŋk]	einen Blackout haben
	chaotic	[keɪ'ɒtɪk]	chaotisch
	commercial director	[kə,mɜːʃl də'rektə]	kaufmännische/r Leiter/in
	chief	[tʃiːf]	Häuptling
	Indian	['ɪndiən]	Indianer/in
	There are too many chiefs and not enough Indians. (coll.)	[ðeə ,tuː meni ,tʃiːfs ənd nɒt ɪnʌf 'ɪndiəns]	Es gibt zu viele Leute, die Befehle erteilen, und nicht genug Leute, die die Arbeit machen.
	area sales manager	[ˌeəriə ˌseɪlz 'mænɪdʒə]	Gebietsverkaufsleiter/in
	let alone	[let ə'ləʊn]	geschweige denn
	recently	['riːsntli]	kürzlich, neulich
	town hall	['taʊn hɔːl]	Rathaus
	suit	[suːt]	Anzug
	head of production	[ˌhed əv prə'dʌkʃn]	Produktionsleiter/in
	to liaise	[li'eɪz]	zusammenarbeiten
	apart from	[ə'pɑːt frəm]	außer
	regional sales manager	[ˌriːdʒənl ˌseɪlz 'mænɪdʒə]	regionale/r Verkaufsleiter/in
	to bear with so	['beə wɪθ]	mit jmdm Geduld haben, mit jmdm nachsichtig sein
	to be in charge of	[bi ɪn 'tʃɑːdʒ əv]	leiten
	lines of reporting	[ˌlaɪnz əv rɪ'pɔːtɪŋ]	Kommunikationskette, Ablauf
	day-to-day	[ˌdeɪ tə 'deɪ]	alltäglich
	acquisition	[ˌækwɪ'zɪʃn]	Akquisition
	sales training	['seɪlz treɪnɪŋ]	Verkaufstraining
	session	['seʃn]	Treffen, Termin
	to grab (coll.)	[græb]	greifen, schnappen
3	to fill in for sb	[fɪl 'ɪn fə]	für jmdn einspringen, jmdn vertreten
	to run	[rʌn]	leiten
	recruitment	[rɪ'kruːtmənt]	Anwerbung, Einstellung
	counterpart	['kaʊntəpɑːt]	Kollege, Kollegin
	MD (= Managing Director)	[em'diː]	Geschäftsführer/in
4	dilemma	[dɪ'lemə]	Dilemma, Verlegenheit
	depth	[depθ]	Stärke, Tiefe
	to feel out of your depth	[fiːl ˌaʊt əv jɔː 'depθ]	überfordert sein
	to quit	[kwɪt]	kündigen, aussteigen
5	impact	['ɪmpækt]	Auswirkung
	integrated	['ɪntɪgreɪtɪd]	eingebunden, integriert
	miner	['maɪnə]	Bergarbeiter/in
	recycler	[ˌriː'saɪklə]	Entsorger, Recycler
	boiler	['bɔɪlə]	Boiler, Heizkessel
	underground	['ʌndəgraʊnd]	unterirdisch

Company structures

a rather hierarchical, ladder-type structure	eine eher hierarchische, leiterartige Struktur
a team-based, flat lattice organization	eine teambasierte Organisation mit flacher Struktur
bureaucratic decision-making processes	bürokratische Entscheidungsprozesse
short chains of command	kurze Anordnungs-/Entscheidungswege
high degrees of individual responsibility	hoher Grad an Eigenverantwortung
fast decision-making capabilities	schnelle Entscheidungsmöglichkeiten
to foster personal initiative	Eigeninitiative unterstützen
to encourage hands-on innovation	zu praktischen Innovationen ermutigen
predetermined channels of communication	festgelegte Kommunikationswege
a rising need for flexibility	ein steigender Bedarf an Flexibilität
to keep the company afloat during a recession	die Firma während einer Rezession über Wasser halten/nicht untergehen lassen
to support team members on an ongoing basis	Teammitglieder/Mitarbeiter kontinuierlich unterstützen
learning-by-doing approach	praxisorientierter Lernansatz / Learning-by-doing-Ansatz
The sun doesn't always shine here, though.	Trotzdem ist hier nicht immer eitel Sonnenschein.

Describing roles and responsibilities

My role/function here is …	Meine Aufgabe/Funktion hier ist …
The scope of my role here is …	Mein Aufgabenbereich hier ist …
I have (overall) responsibility for …	Ich habe die (Gesamt-)Verantwortung für …
I liaise/cooperate with …	Ich arbeite mit … zusammen.
I head (up) / look after a department.	Ich leite / kümmere mich um eine Abteilung.
I report to / work closely with / support …	Ich unterstehe / arbeite eng mit … zusammen / unterstütze …

6	to source	[sɔːs]	beziehen
7	sales order processing	[ˌseɪlz ɔːdə ˈprəʊsesɪŋ]	Auftragsabwicklung
	to submit	[səbˈmɪt]	einreichen
	file	[faɪl]	Akte, Datei
	drawing	[ˈdrɔːɪŋ]	Zeichnung
	to perform	[pəˈfɔːm]	ausführen, vollziehen, erfüllen
	precise	[prɪˈsaɪs]	präzise, genau
	to drill	[ˈdrɪl]	bohren
	to streamline	[ˈstriːmlaɪn]	rationalisieren, beschleunigen
	lead time	[ˈliːd taɪm]	Herstellungszeit
	to combine	[kəmˈbaɪn]	kombinieren, verbinden

| business unit manager | ['bɪznəs juːnɪt mænɪdʒə] | Leiter/in des Geschäftsbereichs |
| sequencing word | ['siːkwənsɪŋ wɜːd] | Gliederungswort |

1C, Management structures

1
layered	['leɪəd]	geschichtet
rigid	['rɪdʒɪd]	starr, unflexibel
contrary	['kɒntrəri]	Gegenteil, Gegensatz
on the contrary	[ɒn ðə 'kɒntrəri]	im Gegenteil
command	[kə'mɑːnd]	Befehl
chain of command	[tʃeɪn əv kə'mɑːnd]	Befehlskette, Dienstweg
capability	[ˌkeɪpə'bɪləti]	Fähigkeit
distinguished	[dɪ'stɪŋgwɪʃt]	angesehen, namhaft
cable assembly	['keɪbl əsembli]	Leitung, Kabelmontage
founding	['faʊndɪŋ]	Gründung
lattice	['lætɪs]	Gitter
to foster	['fɒstə]	fördern, verstärken
predetermined	[ˌpriːdɪ'tɜːmɪnd]	im Voraus bestimmt/festgelegt
channel	['tʃænl]	Kanal, Sender
channel of communication	[ˌtʃænl əv kəˌmjuːnɪ'keɪʃn]	Kommunikationsweg
hands-on	[ˌhændz 'ɒn]	praktisch, praxisnah
to emerge	[i'mɜːdʒ]	herausbringen, hervorbringen
ladder	['lædə]	Leiter
to rank	[ræŋk]	einstufen
ranking	['ræŋkɪŋ]	Einstufung
to favour sth	['feɪvə]	etw vorziehen
to contribute	[kən'trɪbjuːt]	beitragen
afloat	[ə'fləʊt]	über Wasser
recession	[rɪ'seʃn]	Rezession
to abandon	[ə'bændən]	aufgeben
attempt	[ə'tempt]	Versuch
formality	[fɔː'mæləti]	Formalität, Förmlichkeit
to result in	[rɪ'zʌlt ɪn]	führen zu
inventory management	[ɪn'vəntri mænɪdʒmənt]	Lagerverwaltung
re-engineered	[ˌriˌendʒɪ'nɪəd]	neustrukturiert, überarbeitet

3	to admire	[əd'maɪə]	bewundern, schätzen
	stiff	[stɪf]	steif
	approach	[ə'prəʊtʃ]	Annäherung
	mentality	[men'tæləti]	Mentalität
	to document	['dɒkjumənt]	dokumentieren, belegen
	to consume	[kən'sjuːm]	verbrauchen
	time-consuming	['taɪm kənsjuːmɪŋ]	zeitraubend
4	to get rid of	[get 'rɪd əv]	loswerden

1, Grammar summary

robot	['rəʊbɒt]	Roboter
to experience	[ɪk'spɪəriəns]	erleben

1, Extra practice

CS	to slip sth in	[slɪp 'ɪn]	etw einfließen lassen
	when in doubt	[wen ɪn 'daʊt]	im Zweifel
	to become comfortable	[bɪ,kʌm 'kʌmftəbl]	sich wohl fühlen

First name or last name?

to be on a 'du' basis	sich duzen
Time has come to use first names.	Es ist an der Zeit, sich mit dem Vornamen anzureden.
Slip the first name into the introduction and carry on the conversation.	Erwähnen Sie den Vornamen, wenn Sie sich einander vorstellen, und fahren Sie mit der Unterhaltung fort.
Ask for permission to get on a first-name basis.	Fragen Sie, ob Sie sich mit dem Vornamen anreden dürfen.
It is always safer to use titles and surnames when in doubt.	Es ist im Zweifelsfall immer sicherer, Titel und Familiennamen zu verwenden.

2A, A new contact

1	How can you tell?	[,haʊ kən ju 'tel]	Woher wissen Sie das?
	with reference to	[wɪð 'refrəns tə]	mit Bezug auf, bezüglich
	to go live	[gəʊ 'laɪv]	online gehen
	minor	['maɪnə]	klein, gering
	traffic	['træfɪk]	Verkehr, Zugriff
	Please accept my apologies for ...	[pliːz ək,sept maɪ ə'pɒlədʒɪz fə]	Bitte entschuldigen Sie, dass ...
	auditor	['ɔːdɪtə]	Rechnungsprüfer/in, Prüfer/in
	for	[fə]	seit
	a couple of	[ə 'kʌpl əv]	ein paar

2	rate	[reɪt]	Rate, Quote
	traffic rate	['træfɪk reɪt]	Zugriffsquote
6	nearby	[ˌnɪə'baɪ]	nahe gelegen
	to **look into sth**	[ˌlʊk 'ɪntə]	etw untersuchen, etw prüfen

Rearranging an appointment

I am writing with reference to our appointment on …	Ich schreibe Ihnen bezüglich unseres Termins am …
I regret to inform you that I will not be able to attend … / that I can't make it to …	Ich muss Ihnen leider mitteilen, dass ich nicht an … teilnehmen kann / dass ich nicht zu … kommen kann.
I'm afraid we will have to cancel the appointment.	Leider werden wir den Termin absagen müssen.
Would it be possible to postpone our meeting / bring our meeting forward?	Wäre es möglich, unser Treffen zu verschieben / unser Treffen vorzuverlegen?
Could I pencil you in for Wednesday at the same time?	Kann ich Sie für Mittwoch zur gleichen Zeit eintragen?
Please let me know by Friday if this alternative suits you.	Bitte lassen Sie mich bis Freitag wissen, ob Ihnen diese Alternative passt.
I look forward to hearing from you soon.	Ich freue mich (darauf), bald von Ihnen zu hören.
Please accept my apologies for changing our appointment at such a short notice.	Bitte entschuldigen Sie die kurzfristige Terminänderung.
Sorry again for the inconvenience.	Entschuldigen Sie nochmals die Umstände.

7	to **keep short**	[kiːp 'ʃɔːt]	knapp halten, kurz halten
8	draft	[drɑːft]	Konzept, Entwurf
	to **ask sb out for dinner**	[ɑːsk ˌaʊt fə 'dɪnə]	jmdn zum Essen einladen
	eve (= evening)	[iːv]	Abend
	alternative	[ɔːl'tɜːnətɪv]	Alternative

Keeping emails short

More to follow.	Mehr in Kürze.
Fingers crossed!	Ich drücke / Wir drücken die Daumen!
btw (by the way)	übrigens
CU (see you)	Bis bald.
Really appreciate it!	Das weiß ich / wissen wir wirklich zu schätzen!
Quick question re …	Kurze Frage bezüglich …
Dinner on Friday eve?	Abendessen am Freitag?

2B, Business small talk

1	shooter	['ʃuːtə]	Schütze, Schützin
	straight	[streɪt]	offen, direkt, unverblümt
	straight shooter	[streɪt 'ʃuːtə]	jemand, der sehr direkt ist
	detective	[dɪ'tektɪv]	Detektiv/in, Kriminalbeamter/-beamtin
	butterfly	['bʌtəflaɪ]	Schmetterling
	social butterfly	[ˌsəʊʃl 'bʌtəflaɪ]	Partygänger/in
	to flow	[fləʊ]	fließen, strömen
	springtime	['sprɪŋtaɪm]	Frühling
	speaking of	['spiːkɪŋ əv]	apropos
	frankly	['fræŋkli]	offen, ehrlich gesagt
2 (1.9)	builder	['bɪldə]	Bauarbeiter/in
	noise	[nɔɪz]	Lärm, Geräusch
	site	[saɪt]	Stelle, Platz
	construction site	[kən'strʌkʃn saɪt]	Baustelle
	pleasure	['pleʒə]	Vergnügen, Freude, Spaß
	My pleasure.	[maɪ 'pleʒə]	Gern., Mit Vergnügen.
	tasty	['teɪsti]	lecker, schmackhaft
	authentic	[ɔː'θentɪk]	echt, originalgetreu
	accident	['æksɪdənt]	Unfall
	field	[fiːld]	Spielfeld, Platz
	ankle	['æŋkl]	Fußknöchel
	out of action	[aʊt əv 'ækʃn]	außer Gefecht
	to slow down	[sləʊ 'daʊn]	verlangsamen
	to recover	[rɪ'kʌvə]	sich erholen
	holiday home	['hɒlədeɪ həʊm]	Ferienhaus, Ferienwohnung
	short break	['ʃɔːt breɪk]	Kurzurlaub
	to mean to do sth	[ˌmiːn tə 'duː]	etw tun wollen, etw vorhaben
	niece	[niːs]	Nichte
	nephew	['nefjuː]	Neffe
3	empathy	['empəθi]	Mitgefühl
4	host	[həʊst]	Gastgeber/in
(1.10)	a minute's walk	[ə 'mɪnɪts wɔːk]	ein Katzensprung
	historic	[hɪ'stɒrɪk]	historisch
	works of art	[ˌwɜːks əv 'ɑːt]	Kunstwerke
	to plan in	[ˌplæn 'ɪn]	einplanen
	old town	[əʊld 'taʊn]	Altstadt
	famous	['feɪməs]	berühmt
	to admit	[əd'mɪt]	zugeben, eingestehen
	to spend	[spend]	verbringen
7	sacred	['seɪkrɪd]	heilig
	obligation	[ˌɒblɪ'geɪʃn]	Verpflichtung, Pflicht
	executor	[ɪg'zekjətə]	Nachlassverwalter/in, Testamentsvollstrecker/in

Anyway, isn't it just beautiful outside? –	Wie dem auch sei, ist heute nicht ein wunder-
It certainly is. / It is, actually.	schöner Tag? – Ja, stimmt.
Whereabouts are you from, by the way?	Woher genau kommen Sie eigentlich?
I've never been to …, have you?	Ich war noch nie in …, Sie?
– No, I haven't, actually.	– Nein, ehrlich gesagt noch nicht.
Where are you off to after dinner?	Wohin gehen Sie nach dem Abendessen?
Speaking of which, …	Wo wir gerade davon reden, …
Quite frankly, …	Ehrlich/Offen gesagt, …
Really? That sounds interesting!	Tatsächlich? Das hört sich interessant an!

2C, Working internationally

❯	custom	['kʌstəm]	Brauch, Gewohnheit, Sitte
1	discovery	[dɪ'skʌvəri]	Entdeckung
	damage	['dæmɪdʒ]	Schaden, Beschädigung
	to prevent	[prɪ'vent]	verhindern
	in terms of	[ɪn 'tɜːmz əv]	im Sinne von
	simulation	[ˌsɪmju'leɪʃn]	Vortäuschung
	case study	['keɪs stʌdi]	Fallstudie
	acceptance	[ək'septəns]	Akzeptanz, Zustimmung
	sensitivity	[ˌsensə'tɪvəti]	Einfühlungsvermögen
	incident	['ɪnsɪdənt]	Vorfall, Zwischenfall
	critical	['krɪtɪkl]	kritisch, entscheidend
	deliverable	[dɪ'lɪvərəbl]	Arbeitsergebnis
	independently	[ˌɪndɪ'pendəntli]	unabhängig, allein
	to underestimate	[ˌʌndər'estɪmeɪt]	unterschätzen
	breakdown	['breɪkdaʊn]	Störung, Zusammenbruch
	milestone	['maɪlstəʊn]	Meilenstein
	to check in	[ˌtʃek 'ɪn]	*hier:* ankommen
	attitude	['ætɪtjuːd]	Einstellung, Haltung
	to behave	[bɪ'heɪv]	sich benehmen, sich verhalten
3	implication	[ˌɪmplɪ'keɪʃn]	Auswirkung, Konsequenz
	clash	[klæʃ]	Zusammenstoß
	culture clash	['kʌltʃə klæʃ]	kultureller Gegensatz
	plate	[pleɪt]	Teller
	politeness	[pə'laɪtnəs]	Höflichkeit
	to improvise	['ɪmprəvaɪz]	improvisieren
4	belief	[bɪ'liːf]	Überzeugung, Glaube
	to attribute	[ə'trɪbjuːt]	zuschreiben
5	optional	['ɒpʃənl]	freiwillig, fakultativ

2, Grammar summary

| cabinet | ['kæbɪnet] | Schrank |
| storage cabinet | ['stɔːrɪdʒ kæbɪnet] | Lagerschrank, Datenschutzschrank |

2, Extra practice

4	to break the ice	[ˌbreɪk ði 'aɪs]	das Eis brechen
	trust	[trʌst]	Vertrauen
	stuffy	[stʌfi]	stickig
	to fill the time	[ˌfɪl ðə 'taɪm]	Zeit überbrücken
	towards	[tə'wɔːds]	(in) Richtung

Making small talk II

Thanks for coming.	Danke, dass Sie gekommen sind.
Thanks for asking us. – My pleasure.	Danke für die Einladung. – Es war mir ein Vergnügen.
It will be my turn to treat you to lunch next time, if I may.	Nächstes Mal würde ich Sie gerne zum Mittagessen einladen, wenn ich darf.

Business file 1 – A company visit

1	business development	[ˌbɪznəs dɪ'veləpment]	Akquisition, Geschäftsentwicklung
1.11	expansion	[ɪk'spænʃn]	Expansion, Erweiterung
	connection	[kə'nekʃn]	Verbindung, Beziehung
	SWOT analysis (SWOT = Strengths, Weaknesses, Opportunities and Threats)	[swɒt ə'næləsɪs]	Stärken-Schwächen-Analyse
	distribution	[ˌdɪstrɪ'bjuːʃn]	Vertrieb
	strategy	['strætədʒi]	Strategie
	trade show	['treɪd ʃəʊ]	Handelsmesse
	sales meeting	['seɪlz miːtɪŋ]	Vertriebsveranstaltung
	specifically	[spə'sɪfɪkli]	speziell, besonders
	particularly	[pə'tɪkjələli]	insbesondere, vor allem
	initially	[ɪ'nɪʃli]	zunächst
	associate	[ə'səʊʃiət]	Kollege, Kollegin, Mitarbeiter/in
	social media	[ˌsəʊʃl 'miːdɪə]	soziale Medien, soziale Netzwerke

Answering a phone call

Thanks for holding. How may I help you?	Danke, dass Sie gewartet haben. Wie kann ich Ihnen helfen?
Thank you for getting back to me so promptly.	Danke, dass Sie so schnell zurückgerufen haben.
I'm ringing to see if we could perhaps …	Ich rufe an um zu klären/fragen, ob wir vielleicht …

2	scene	[si:n]	Szene
3	debrief	[ˌdiː'briːf]	Zusammenfassung, (nach) Besprechung
4	hospitality	[ˌhɒspɪ'tælɪti]	Gastfreundschaft
	awful	['ɔːfl]	schrecklich
	quite a bit	[ˌkwaɪt ə 'bɪt]	ziemlich viel
	lovely	['lʌvli]	schön, herrlich
	scenery	['siːnəri]	Landschaft

A company visit

Meeting a visitor / Arriving at a company

Nice to meet you (at last).	Schön, Sie (endlich) kennenzulernen.
How are you?	Wie geht es Ihnen?
Welcome to … Did you have a good journey/flight?	Willkommen bei/in … Hatten Sie eine angenehme Reise / einen angenehmen Flug?
Would you like to come this way? / Would you like to follow me?	Würden Sie bitte hier entlang mitkommen? / Würden Sie mir bitte hier entlang folgen?
It's a nice office you have here.	Ein schönes Büro haben Sie hier.
May I / Can I take your coat?	Darf ich Ihnen den Mantel abnehmen?
Could I use your toilet, please? – The toilets are over there / along the corridor / just through there on the right/left.	Entschuldigen Sie, wo sind bitte die Toiletten? – Die Toiletten sind dort drüben / den Flur entlang / einfach dort durch auf der rechten/ linken Seite.
May I / Can I introduce …? / I don't think you know … – Pleased to meet you.	Darf ich Ihnen … vorstellen? / Ich glaube, Sie haben … noch nicht kennengelernt. – Freut mich, Sie kennenzulernen.
Would you like / Can I offer you a cup of tea/coffee? – I'd prefer some water, if you have it.	Möchten Sie eine Tasse Tee/Kaffee? / Darf ich Ihnen eine Tasse Tee/Kaffee anbieten? – Ich hätte bitte lieber Wasser, wenn das geht.

Getting to know your visitors/hosts

Is this your first visit to …?	Ist dies Ihr erster Aufenthalt in …?
Not quite – I've been here once.	Nicht ganz – ich war schon einmal hier.
How long have you been with your company?	Wie lange arbeiten Sie schon bei Ihrem Unternehmen?
Three years. Before that I was / worked for …	Drei Jahre. Vorher war ich … / habe ich für … gearbeitet.
Do you travel a lot on your job?	Sind Sie beruflich viel unterwegs?

Getting down to business

Shall we get started/make a start?	Sollen wir beginnen?
Is everyone ready?	Sind alle soweit?
Would you like to take a seat? / Would you like to sit over here?	Möchten Sie Platz nehmen? / Möchten Sie hier sitzen?
The programme that we've worked out for today is ... Does that sound OK?	Das Programm, das wir für heute ausgearbeitet haben, ist ... Sind Sie damit einverstanden?
We've prepared an information pack for you.	Wir haben Ihnen einige Informationen zusammengestellt.
Perhaps we could go round the table and everyone could introduce themselves.	Vielleicht können wir eine Vorstellungsrunde machen.
Could you tell us a little more about your company?	Könnten Sie uns ein bisschen mehr über Ihr Unternehmen erzählen?

3A, New plans

▶ B2B = Business-to-business [ˌbiː tə 'biː] Geschäftsbeziehungen zwischen Unternehmen

transaction	[trænˈzækʃn]	Geschäft, Transaktion
1 to comply with sth	[kəmˈplaɪ wɪð]	etw befolgen
to tender	[ˈtendə]	ein Angebot einreichen
call for tenders	[ˌkɔːl fə ˈtendəz]	Ausschreibung
invitation to tender	[ɪnvɪˌteɪʃn tə ˈtendə]	Ausschreibung (Preis)
tender	[ˈtendə]	Angebot

Invitation to tender

call for tenders/invitation to tender/ request for proposal (RFP)	Ausschreibung
... is due to open in ...	... soll am/im ... eröffnen
the medium-term plan calls for ...	der mittelfristige Plan sieht ... vor
a total of ...	insgesamt ...
Tender must be submitted in compliance with the attended documents.	Das Angebot muss in Übereinstimmung mit den beiliegenden Dokumenten eingereicht werden.
It is the responsibility of the tenderers to ensure that submissions are received by ...	Für die fristgerechte Einsendung bis zum ... sind die Bieter verantwortlich.

call	[kɔːl]	Aufruf
help desk	[ˈhelp desk]	Informationsdienst, Support Anwenderunterstützung
point of sale	[ˌpɔɪnt əv ˈseɪl]	Verkaufsstelle
setting up	[ˌsetɪŋ ˈʌp]	das Einrichten
medium-term	[ˈmiːdiəm tɜːm]	mittelfristig

	to call for	['kɔːl fə]	erfordern, verlangen
	retail operator	[riːteɪl 'ɒpəreɪtə]	Einzelhändler/in
	in compliance with	[ɪn kəm'plaɪəns wɪð]	gemäß
3	move	[muːv]	Schritt
🔊 1.12	subcontractor	[ˌsʌbkən'træktə]	Subunternehmer/in
	to set up	[set 'ʌp]	errichten
	bell	[bel]	Glocke
	to ring a bell *(coll.)*	[rɪŋ ə 'bel]	bekannt vorkommen
	to go for sb	['gəʊ fə]	sich für jmdn entscheiden
	to score	[skɔː]	Punkte erzielen
	criteria	[kraɪ'tɪəriə]	Kriterien
	checklist	['tʃeklɪst]	Checkliste, Prüfliste
	far off	[fɑːr 'ɒf]	fern, weit entfernt
	cash register	['kæʃ redʒɪstə]	Kasse
	to appoint	[ə'pɔɪnt]	ernennen
	elsewhere	[ˌels'weə]	anderswo
	to have sb in mind	[həv ɪn 'maɪnd]	an jmdn denken
4	prior	['praɪə]	früher, vorherig
6	to send one's apologies	[ˌsend wʌnz ə'pɒlədʒiz]	sich entschuldigen lassen
🔊 1.13	to mute	[mjuːt]	(ein Gerät) auf „stumm" schalten
	to dial in	[daɪəl 'ɪn]	einwählen
	to speak up	[spiːk 'ʌp]	lauter sprechen
	up and running	[ˌʌp ən 'rʌnɪŋ]	in Gang, funktionierend
	present	['preznt]	anwesend
	to indicate	['ɪndɪkeɪt]	zu verstehen geben, anzeigen
	to exclude	[ɪk'skluːd]	ausschließen
	possibility	[ˌpɒsə'bɪləti]	Möglichkeit
	Do you follow me?	[duː ju 'fɒləʊ mi]	Können Sie mir folgen?, Verstehen Sie?
	trade union	[ˌtreɪd 'juːniən]	Gewerkschaft
	training provider	['treɪnɪŋ prəvaɪdə]	Anbieter von Weiterbildungen
	to develop	[dɪ'veləp]	aufbauen, *hier:* schulen
	scope	[skəʊp]	Bereich, Umfang, Rahmen
	to be beyond the scope of sth	[bi bɪ,jɒnd ðə 'skəʊp əv]	außerhalb des Rahmens von etw liegen, den Rahmen von etw sprengen
	call	[kɔːl]	Gespräch
	That's fine with me.	[ðæts 'faɪn wɪð mi]	In Ordnung., Einverstanden.
7	to happen to do	['hæpən tə duː]	etw zufällig tun
🔊 1.14	to pass on	[pɑːs 'ɒn]	weitergeben
	to eliminate sb	[ɪ'lɪmɪneɪt]	jmdn ausschließen
	to move on	[muːv 'ɒn]	weitermachen, fortfahren
	brief	[briːf]	Briefing, Einweisung
	to come in	[kʌm 'ɪn]	*hier:* sich einschalten
	Pardon?	['pɑːdn]	Wie bitte?
	successful	[sək'sesfl]	erfolgreich
	rope	[rəʊp]	Seil, Tau
	to learn the ropes *(coll.)*	[lɜːn ðə 'rəʊps]	sich einarbeiten, die Basics lernen
	to fill	[fɪl]	*hier:* Stelle besetzen

backwards	['bækwədz]	rückwärts, von hinten nach vorn
retail staff	['riːteɪl stɑːf]	Verkaufspersonal
rolling start	['rəʊlɪŋ stɑːt]	Start aus einem fortlaufenden Projekt
capacity	[kə'pæsəti]	Kapazität, Leistungsvermögen
over the course of	[əʊvə ðə 'kɔːs əv]	im Verlauf von; im Laufe von; innerhalb von
to reach capacity	[ˌriːtʃ kə'pæsəti]	mit voller Leistung arbeiten
per cent	[pə 'sent]	Prozent
parallel	['pærəlel]	parallel
recruitment drive	[rɪ'kruːtmənt draɪv]	Einstellungsverfahren
to cover	['kʌvə]	abdecken
to participate	[pɑː'tɪsɪpeɪt]	teilnehmen
productive	[prə'dʌktɪv]	ergebnisreich, produktiv
done	[dʌn]	fertig, erledigt
to send off	[send 'ɒf]	wegschicken
action plan	['ækʃn plæn]	Maßnahmenplan
to hold an interview	[həʊld ən 'ɪntəvjuː]	ein Vorstellungsgespräch/ Bewerbungsgespräch führen
to equip	[ɪ'kwɪp]	ausstatten, ausrüsten
in parallel	[ɪn 'pærəlel]	parallel dazu
curious	['kjʊəriəs]	neugierig

Talking to B2B-partners

Things are moving fast.	Die Dinge entwickeln sich schnell.
The name rings a bell, but I'm not sure.	Der Name sagt mir etwas, aber ich bin mir nicht sicher.
Why did you go for them? – They scored the most points on our checklist.	Warum haben Sie sich für diese Firma entschieden? – Sie entspricht unseren Vorstellungen am meisten.
When do you want to have the conference call? – I was thinking first thing on Monday.	Wann möchten Sie die Telefonkonferenz machen? – Ich dachte gleich am Montagmorgen.
I won't be in my office until mid-morning at the earliest.	Ich werde frühestens am späten Vormittag im Büro sein.

8	face-to-face	[ˌfeɪs tə 'feɪs]	von Angesicht zu Angesicht, persönlich
	to lead in	[liːd 'ɪn]	einleiten
	set phrase	['set freɪz]	Floskel, Formel
	to take it in turns	[ˌteɪk ɪt ɪn 'tɜːns]	sich abwechseln
	set	[set]	*hier:* fertig, bereit
9	to keep to sth	['kiːp tə]	sich an etw halten
	time limit	['taɪm lɪmɪt]	Zeitvorgabe, zeitlicher Rahmen
	to put forward	[ˌpʊt 'fɔːwəd]	vorschlagen, vortragen
	to think up	[ˌθɪŋk 'ʌp]	sich ausdenken, erfinden
	every now and then	[evri ˌnaʊ ən 'ðen]	hin und wieder, gelegentlich
	clarification	[ˌklærəfɪ'keɪʃn]	Klärung, Klarstellung
	relative	['relətɪv]	Verwandte/r
	to support	[sə'pɔːt]	unterstützen
	public transport	[ˌpʌblɪk 'trænspɔːt]	öffentliche Verkehrsmittel

group discount	[ˌgruːp 'dɪskaʊnt]	Gruppenrabatt
to **shout**	[ʃaʊt]	schreien, brüllen
volume	['vɒljuːm]	Lautstärke, Volumen
data projector	[ˌdeɪtə prə'dʒektə]	Beamer
Did I make myself clear?	[dɪd aɪ ˌmeɪk maɪself 'klɪə]	Haben Sie mich verstanden?, Habe ich mich verständlich ausgedrückt?
idiom	['ɪdiəm]	Redewendung, idiomatische Wendung
to **go on** sth	['gəʊ ɒn]	sich auf etw stützen
enthusiasm	[ɪn'θjuːziæzəm]	Begeisterung, Enthusiasmus
key point	['kiː pɔɪnt]	springender Punkt, Schwerpunkt

Conducting a conference call

I'd like to check that everybody is connected. All right, we're all set.	Ich würde gerne überprüfen, ob alle verbunden sind. Alles klar, es sind alle da.
He sends his apologies. He can't be with us today.	Er lässt sich entschuldigen. Er kann heute leider nicht dabei sein.
Bear with me. I need to dial him in again.	Einen Moment bitte. Ich muss ihn nochmal einwählen.
Could you speak up / slow down please? It's hard to hear you.	Könnten Sie bitte lauter / langsamer sprechen? Sie sind schlecht zu verstehen.
Sorry, I didn't quite catch that. Do you mean …?	Entschuldigung, das habe ich nicht ganz verstanden. Meinen Sie …?
That topic is beyond the scope of today's agenda. Let's return to it at our next call.	Dieses Thema steht heute nicht auf der Tagesordnung. Lassen Sie und bei unserer nächsten Telefonkonferenz darauf zurückkommen.
I think that more or less covers everything for today.	Ich denke, das ist im Großen und Ganzen alles für heute.
Thank you for participating.	Vielen Dank für Ihre Teilnahme.

Interrupting

He jumped into the conversation.	Er unterbrach das Gespräch.
Sorry to interrupt. Can I just say something here?	Entschuldigen Sie, dass ich Sie unterbreche. Könnte ich kurz etwas sagen?
Excuse me, I'd just like to say …	Entschuldigen Sie, ich wollte nur sagen, dass …
May I just finish my point?	Könnte ich mein Argument zu Ende ausführen?
Sorry, I didn't realize you weren't finished. Please go on!	Entschuldigung, mir war nicht bewusst, dass Sie noch nicht fertig sind. Bitte fahren Sie fort!
I beg your pardon. Please continue.	Entschuldigung. Fahren Sie bitte fort.
Can/Could I just come in here?	Kann ich hier kurz unterbrechen?
Sorry, I need to stop you here.	Entschuldigung, ich muss Sie hier unterbrechen.

3B, Moving forward

▶	to move forward	[ˌmuːv ˈfɔːwəd]	vorankommen
1	progress report	[ˈprəʊgres rɪpɔːt]	Lagebericht, Zwischenbericht
	executive summary	[ɪgˈzekjətɪv sʌməri]	Kurzdarstellung, Zusammenfassung
	distribution	[ˌdɪstrɪˈbjuːʃn]	*hier:* Verteiler, Verteilung
	in line with	[ɪn ˈlaɪn wɪð]	im Rahmen, in Übereinstimmung mit
	to date	[tə ˈdeɪt]	bisher

Organizing your tasks

The project is in line with its objectives.	Die im Projekt festgesetzten Ziele werden erreicht.
The milestones have nearly all been reached.	Es wurden fast alle Meilensteine erreicht.
… is clearly shown in the detailed description of …	… zeigt sich deutlich in der genauen Beschreibung von/der/des …
Here follows an executive summary of …	Hier/Es folgt eine Kurzdarstellung von/der/des …

2	to fax	[fæks]	faxen, per Fax senden
	to be of bad quality	[bi əv ˌbæd ˈkwɒləti]	von schlechter Qualität sein
	to prove to be sth	[ˈpruːv tə bi]	sich als etw erweisen
	vacancy	[ˈveɪkənsi]	offene Stelle
	meantime	[ˈmiːntaɪm]	Zwischenzeit
	in working order	[ɪn ˈwɜːkɪŋ ɔːdə]	in betriebsfähigem Zustand
3	criticism	[ˈkrɪtɪsɪzəm]	Kritik
4	at first hand	[ət ˈfɜːst hænd]	aus erster Hand
🔊 1.15	payment system	[ˈpeɪmənt sɪstəm]	Zahlungssystem
	retail outlet	[ˈriːteɪl aʊtlet]	Einzelhandelsgeschäft, Ladengeschäft
	skill set	[ˈskɪl set]	Anforderungsprofil
	working knowledge	[ˈwɜːkɪŋ nɒlɪdʒ]	Grundkenntnisse
	payment gateway	[ˈpeɪmənt geɪtweɪ]	Zahlungsportal
	service provider	[ˈsɜːvɪs prəvaɪdə]	Dienstleister
	practice	[ˈpræktɪs]	Vorgehensweise, Praxis
	bilingual	[ˌbaɪlɪŋgwəl]	zweisprachig
	oral	[ˈɔːrəl]	mündlich
	perspective	[pəˈspektɪv]	Perspektive, Blickwinkel
	to come to the table with	[kʌm tə ðə ˈteɪbl wɪð]	etw mitbringen
	to prioritize	[praɪˈɒrətaɪz]	Prioritäten setzen, der Wichtigkeit nach ordnen
	to pick up sth	[ˌpɪk ˈʌp]	sich etw aneignen
	to turn around	[ˌtɜːn əˈraʊnd]	wenden, umdrehen
	supportive	[səˈpɔːtɪv]	hilfreich, unterstützend
	prospect	[ˈprɒspekt]	Aussicht
	contribution	[ˌkɒntrɪˈbjuːʃn]	Beitrag
	starting date	[ˈstɑːtɪŋ deɪt]	Einstellungsdatum

competency	['kɒmpɪtənsi]	Kompetenz, Fähigkeit
equivalent	[ɪ'kwɪvələnt]	Pendant, Äquivalent
physical	['fɪzɪkl]	materiell, stofflich
point of sale terminal	[ˌpɔɪnt əv 'seɪl tɜːmɪnl]	Kasse
7 to jot sth down	[dʒɒt 'daʊn]	etw notieren
to widen	['waɪdn]	erweitern
to enhance	[ɪn'hɑːns]	stärken, verbessern
to enable	[ɪ'neɪbl]	ermöglichen
8 well-known	[ˌwel 'nəʊn]	bekannt
proverb	['prɒvɜːb]	Sprichwort
saying	['seɪɪŋ]	Redensart

Talking about your experience, skills and knowledge

I have experience in / a good knowledge of / a good track record in …	Ich habe Erfahrungen mit / kenne mich gut aus mit / Erfolg gehabt mit …
I have the right skill set and the relevant experience.	Ich habe die richtigen Voraussetzungen und die nötige Erfahrung.
I have qualifications / a diploma / a degree in …	Ich habe Zeugnisse von / ein Diplom in / einen Abschluss in …
My experience in my job has enabled me to …	Meine Berufserfahrung ermöglicht es mir, …
One of my biggest strengths is …	Eine meiner größten Stärken ist …
As for weaknesses, I must admit …	Was Schwächen angeht, muss ich zugeben, dass …
I'm quick at picking up things / eager to learn new things.	Ich habe eine schnelle Auffassungsgabe / möchte sehr gerne neue Dinge lernen.
I work well under pressure.	Ich bin belastbar.
I am able to lead a team/ not afraid of meeting new challenges.	Ich kann ein Team leiten / stelle mich gerne neuen Herausforderungen.
This is one area I'd like to improve on.	Auf diesem Gebiet würde ich mich gerne verbessern.

3C, Team building

1 team-building	['tiːm bɪldɪŋ]	Teamentwicklung
to unwind	[ˌʌn'waɪnd]	sich entspannen, abschalten
motorized	['məʊtəraɪzd]	motorisiert
crystal	['krɪstl]	Kristall
celebration	[ˌselɪ'breɪʃn]	Feier
themed	[θiːmd]	Themen-, themenorientiert
specialist	['speʃəlɪst]	Spezial-, Fach-
to lay out sth	[ˌleɪ 'aʊt]	gestalten, auslegen
to award	[ə'wɔːd]	verleihen
ethos	['iːθɒs]	Ethos
design	[dɪ'zaɪn]	Gestaltung, Konzeption
giant	['dʒaɪənt]	riesig
canvas	['kænvəs]	Leinwand
stack	[stæk]	Haufen, Stapel

to divide up	[dɪ,vaɪd 'ʌp]	aufteilen
mural	['mjʊərəl]	Wandgemälde
fist	[fɪst]	Faust
to enter	['entə]	eintreten
to gamble	['gæmblə]	spielen, wetten
to try one's luck	[,traɪ wʌnz 'lʌk]	sein Glück versuchen
blackjack	['blækdʒæk]	*Kartenspiel:* Siebzehnundvier
to have a flutter on (*coll.*)	[həv ə 'flʌtər ɒn]	*Wette:* sein Glück versuchen
roulette wheel	[ru:'let wi:l]	Roulette
complement	['kɒmplɪmənt]	Ergänzung, Vervollständigung
Parmesan	['pɑːmɪzæn]	Parmesan
script	[skrɪpt]	Drehbuch
adventure	[əd'ventʃə]	Abenteuer
to come away with	[kʌm ə'weɪ]	(mit etw) gehen, mitnehmen
helicopter	['helɪkɒptə]	Hubschrauber
speedboat	['spiːdbəʊt]	Motorboot, Schnellboot
stock	[stɒk]	Aktie
intricate	['ɪntrɪkət]	kompliziert
scandal	['skændl]	Skandal, Klatsch
large screen	[,lɑːdʒ 'skriːn]	Großbildschirm, Großbildleinwand
interest	['ɪntrəst]	Zinsen

3
🔊 **1.16**

countryside	['kʌntrisaɪd]	Landschaft, Natur
grounds	[graʊndz]	Gelände, Parkanlage
puzzle	['pʌzl]	Rätsel, Puzzle
prize	[praɪz]	Preis
egg	[eg]	Ei
to involve	[ɪn'vɒlv]	mit sich bringen, zur Folge haben, be-inhalten
wet	[wet]	nass
to swing	[swɪŋ]	schwingen, baumeln
celebrity	[sə'lebrəti]	berühmte Persönlichkeit
jungle	['dʒʌŋgl]	Dschungel
mobile	['məʊbaɪl]	mobil
to freak out	[friːk 'aʊt]	ausflippen
to climb up	[klaɪm 'ʌp]	hochklettern
distressed	[dɪ'strest]	beunruhigt, verunsichert
confidence	['kɒnfɪdəns]	Vertrauen, Selbstvertrauen
to overcome	[,əʊvə'kʌm]	überwinden
fear	[fɪə]	Angst
to tend to sth	[tend tə]	zu etw neigen, zu etw tendieren
in control	[ɪn kən'trəʊl]	unter Kontrolle
to feel part of	[fiːl 'pɑːt əv]	sich als Teil fühlen
proper	['prɒpə]	richtig, anständig

3, Extra practice

5	ambitious	[æm'bɪʃəs]	ehrgeizig, ambitioniert
9	adviser	[əd'vaɪzə]	Berater/in
CS	to interview	['ɪntəvjuː]	ein Vorstellungsgespräch führen
	concise	[kən'saɪs]	prägnant, knapp
	opening	['əʊpənɪŋ]	erste/r/s; einleitend
	opening	['əʊpənɪŋ]	Eröffnungs-
	to keep on the track	[ˌkiːp ɒn ðə 'træk]	in der Spur bleiben
	to waffle (coll.)	['wɒfl]	schwafeln
	curve	[kɜːv]	Kurve
	to throw a curve ball	[ˌθrəʊ ə 'kɜːv bɔːl]	(mit einer Frage) überrumpeln
	to pause	[pɔːz]	pausieren, innehalten
	to paraphrase	['pærəfreɪz]	anders ausdrücken, umschreiben
	to gather one's thoughts	[ˌgæðə wʌnz 'θɔːts]	seine Gedanken sammeln
	silence	['saɪləns]	Stille
	to put the ball in sb's court	[put ðə 'bɔːl ɪn sʌmbədis 'kɔːt]	jmdm den Ball zuwerfen/zuspielen

Making a good impression in interviews

Don't get off the point.	Schweifen Sie nicht ab.
Opening structures will keep you on track and reduce waffling.	Mit einer klaren Struktur behalten Sie den Überblick und schweifen nicht vom Thema ab.
Somebody might throw you a curve ball.	Jemand könnte Sie überrumpeln (wollen).
Put the ball into his court.	Spielen Sie ihm den Ball zu.

4A, A company help desk

1	to cooperate	[kəʊ'ɒpereɪt]	kooperieren
	daytime	['deɪtaɪm]	Tag
	to fix	[fɪks]	reparieren
	prompt	[prɒmpt]	prompt, unverzüglich
	imaging machine	['ɪmɪdʒɪŋ məʃiːn]	MRT-Gerät, Röntgengerät
	laser	['leɪzə]	Laser
	healthcare	['helθkeə]	Gesundheitsversorgung, Gesundheitspflege
	supply	[sə'plaɪ]	Mittel
	field visit	['fiːld vɪzɪt]	Vor-Ort-Termin, Kundenbesuch
	loan equipment	['ləʊn ɪkwɪpmənt]	Geräteverleih
	preventative	[prɪ'ventətɪv]	Präventiv-, vorbeugend
	check	[tʃek]	Überprüfung, Kontrolle
	preventative check	[prɪˌventətɪv 'tʃek]	Wartung
	to malfunction	[mæl'fʌŋkʃən]	nicht richtig funktionieren
	to readjust	['riːə'dʒʌst]	neu einstellen, nachstellen
	to stand by	[stænd 'baɪ]	zur Verfügung stehen, bereitstehen

	24/7	[ˌtwentiˌfɔː ˈsevən]	24 Stunden, 7 Tage die Woche
	dial-in	[ˌdaɪəl ˈɪn]	telefonisch, Anruf-
	diagnostic	[ˌdaɪəgˈnɒstɪk]	diagnostisch
	diagnostic support	[ˌdaɪəgˌnɒstɪk səˈpɔːt]	Hilfe bei der Fehlersuche, Fehleranalyse
	maintenance	[ˈmeɪntənəns]	Instandhaltung, Wartung
	sound	[saʊnd]	solide, vernünftig, fest
	prevention	[prɪˈvenʃn]	Vorbeugung, Schutz
	tailor	[ˈteɪlə]	Schneider/in
	tailor-made	[ˌteɪlə ˈmeɪd]	zugeschnitten, passgenau
	testimonial	[ˌtestɪˈməʊniəl]	Kundenbewertung, Testimonial
	to assign sb	[əˈsaɪn]	jmdn beauftragen, jmdn zuteilen
3	performance rating	[pəˈfɔːməns reɪtɪŋ]	Leistungsbewertung
4	lately	[ˈleɪtli]	in letzter Zeit
🔊 1.18	at all	[ət ˈɔːl]	überhaupt
	to show up	[ˌʃəʊ ˈʌp]	auftauchen, erscheinen
	receipt	[rɪˈsiːt]	Quittung
	outdated	[ˌaʊtˈdeɪtɪd]	veraltet, nicht mehr aktuell
	manual	[ˈmænjuəl]	handgeschrieben, handschriftlich
	at once	[ət ˈwʌns]	sofort
	warranty	[ˈwɒrənti]	Garantie
	truth	[truːθ]	Wahrheit
	rude	[ruːd]	unhöflich
	fed up	[ˌfed ˈʌp]	genervt
	to take up	[ˌteɪk ˈʌp]	beanspruchen
	to lead to	[liːd tə]	*hier:* führen zu
	traffic jam	[ˈtræfɪk dʒæm]	Verkehrsstau
	cause	[kɔːz]	Grund, Ursache

Cause and effect

The equipment is faulty, so we can't deliver by the deadline.	Die Ausstattung ist fehlerhaft, deshalb können wir nicht fristgerecht liefern.
Our office is being reorganized and as a result of this, …	Unser Büro wird umstrukturiert, deshalb …
Last night's storm led to … and has caused …	Der Sturm letzte Nacht führte zu … und verursachte …
The mistake was due to a misunderstanding.	Der Fehler passierte aufgrund eines Missverständnisses.
… made the customer angry, which meant we lost the order.	… verärgerte den Kunden, was bedeutete, dass wir den Auftrag verloren.

6	improper	[ɪmˈprɒpə]	unsachgemäß
	misunderstanding	[ˌmɪsʌndəˈstændɪŋ]	Missverständnis, Meinungsverschiedenheit
7	to come through	[ˌkʌm ˈθruː]	durchkommen
8	linking word	[ˈlɪŋkɪŋ wɜːd]	Verbindungswort
	to pay a visit	[ˌpeɪ ə ˈvɪzɪt]	einen Besuch abstatten
	to be in a hurry	[bi ɪn ə ˈhʌri]	in Eile sein, es eilig haben

to pay attention	[peɪ əˈtenʃn]	aufpassen, aufmerksam sein
9 to assess	[əˈses]	einschätzen, beurteilen
sympathy	[ˈsɪmpəθi]	Verständnis, Mitgefühl, Unterstützung
to mop	[mɒp]	wischen
caution	[ˈkɔːʃn]	Vorsicht, Warnung
instrument	[ˈɪnstrəmənt]	Instrument, Gerät
to slip	[slɪp]	ausrutschen
to hit the floor	[ˌhɪt ðə ˈflɔː]	auf den Boden fallen
knee	[niː]	Knie
to limp	[lɪmp]	hinken, humpeln
injury	[ˈɪndʒəri]	Verletzung
by mistake	[baɪ mɪˈsteɪk]	aus Versehen
to crowd around	[ˌkraʊd əˈraʊnd]	sich drängen
lap	[læp]	Schoß
to stand in for sb	[ˌstænd ˈɪn fə]	für jmdn einspringen
to deputize for sb	[ˈdepjutaɪz fə]	für jmdn einspringen
to substitute	[ˈsʌbstɪtjuːt]	ersetzen, vertreten

4B, A weekly task force meeting

1 task force	[ˈtɑːsk fɔːs]	Arbeitsgruppe
to reach a decision	[ˌriːtʃ ə dɪˈsɪʒn]	zu einer Entscheidung kommen, entschließen
perception	[pəˈsepʃn]	Wahrnehmung, Verständnis
reward	[rɪˈwɔːd]	Belohnung
CSR = customer service representative	[ˌsiː es ˈɑː]	Kundenberater/in
remotely	[rɪˈməʊtli]	entfernt, im Geringsten
to treat sb	[triːt]	jmdn behandeln
to respect	[rɪˈspekt]	respektieren, achten
harsh	[hɑːʃ]	hart, harsch
to navigate	[ˈnævɪgeɪt]	navigieren, bedienen
hardly	[ˈhɑːdli]	kaum
up to a point	[ˌʌp tu ə ˈpɔɪnt]	bis zu einem bestimmten Punkt
to run into problems	[ˌrʌn ɪntə ˈprɒbləms]	Probleme bekommen
occasion	[əˈkeɪʒn]	Gelegenheit, Anlass, Ereignis
absolutely	[ˈæbsəluːtli]	absolut, sicher
feasibility	[ˌfiːzəˈbɪləti]	Machbarkeit, Durchführbarkeit
to desire	[dɪˈzaɪə]	wünschen
attendance	[əˈtendəns]	Anwesenheit, Teilnehmerzahl
compulsory	[kəmˈpʌlsəri]	obligatorisch, Pflicht-
vote	[vəʊt]	Abstimmung
to be in favour of sth	[bi ɪn ˈfeɪvə əv]	für etw sein
abstention	[əbˈstenʃn]	Stimmenthaltung, Enthaltung
partial	[ˈpɑːʃl]	teilweise, partiell
tentative	[ˈtentətɪv]	zaghaft, zögernd
2 substitute	[ˈsʌbstɪtjuːt]	Ersatz
3 among	[əˈmʌŋ]	zwischen, unter, inmitten

🔊 1.19

	ought to	['ɔːt tu]	sollen
	to entitle sb to sth	[ɪn'taɪtl tə]	jmdn zu etw berechtigen
4	smoker	['sməʊkə]	Raucher/in
	ease	[iːz]	Entspanntheit, Gelassenheit

Agreeing and disagreeing I

I (don't) think/believe …	Ich denke/glaube (nicht) …
I'm afraid I have to disagree.	Leider kann ich nicht zustimmen.
I see your point, but …	Ich verstehe Ihren Standpunkt, aber …
That's a very good point, but …	Das ist ein sehr gutes Argument, aber …
Actually, I'm not really sure.	Ehrlich gesagt bin ich nicht ganz sicher.
That may be the case.	Das könnte der Fall sein.
It has been decided to …	Es wurde entschieden, …
It was agreed to …	Man hat vereinbart, …
It was found that …	Es kam heraus, dass …

5	incentive	[ɪn'sentɪv]	Anreiz
	regardless of	[rɪ'gɑːdləs ɒf]	ungeachtet, ohne Rücksicht auf
	to award	[ə'wɔːd]	*hier:* zuerkennen
6	cut	[kʌt]	Kürzung, Schnitt
1.20	outsourcing	['aʊtsɔːsɪŋ]	Ausgliederung, Auslagerung
	way *(coll.)*	[weɪ]	viel
	to outsource	['aʊtsɔːs]	ausgliedern, auslagern
1.21	history	['hɪstri]	*hier:* Verlauf
	incoming	['ɪnkʌmɪŋ]	eingehend, ankommend
	to enhance the code	[ɪnhɑːns ðə kəʊd]	den Code verbessern
1.22	to fill sb in on sth	[fɪl 'ɪn ɒn]	jmdn über etw informieren
	obstacle	['ɒbstəkl]	Hindernis, Schwierigkeit
	in-depth	[ˌɪn'depθ]	detailliert, eingehend, gründlich
	behaviour	[bɪ'heɪvjə]	Benehmen, Verhalten
	to commission	[kə'mɪʃn]	in Auftrag geben, beauftragen
	to record	[rɪ'kɔːd]	dokumentieren, aufzeichnen
7	wording	['wɜːdɪŋ]	Formulierung
	accidentally	[ˌæksɪ'dentəli]	versehentlich
	to clear up	[ˌklɪər 'ʌp]	aufklären
	to strike	[straɪk]	schlagen, treffen
	iron	['aɪən]	Eisen
	Strike while the iron's hot.	[straɪk waɪl ði ˌaɪənz 'hɒt]	Man muss das Eisen schmieden, solange es heiß ist.

4C, Meetings

1	integral	['ɪntɪgrəl]	wesentlich
	irrelevant	[ɪ'reləvənt]	irrelevant, unwichtig
	occasionally	[ə'keɪʒnəli]	gelegentlich, hin und wieder
	fairly	['feəli]	ziemlich, relativ
	to ban	[bæn]	verbieten, sperren
	to daydream	['deɪdriːm]	mit offenen Augen träumen, tagträumen
	shopping list	['ʃɒpɪŋ lɪst]	Einkaufsliste
	to fall asleep	[ˌfɒl ə'sliːp]	einschlafen
2	to allocate	['æləkeɪt]	bestimmen, zuweisen
	to bring sth to sb's attention	[ˌbrɪŋ tu ə'tenʃn]	jmdn auf etw aufmerksam machen
	comfort	['kʌmfət]	Behaglichkeit, Komfort
	comfort break	['kʌmfət breɪk]	kurze Pause
	consensus	[kən'sensəs]	Übereinstimmung, Einigung
	to reach consensus	[ˌriːtʃ kən'sensəs]	Übereinstimmung erzielen, sich einigen
	to bond	[bɒnd]	*hier:* verbinden, zusammenschweißen
	to impart	[ɪm'pɑːt]	mitteilen, vermitteln
	adequate	['ædɪkwət]	ausreichend, angemessen
	timeliness	['taɪmlinəs]	Rechtzeitigkeit, Pünktlichkeit
	assumption	[ə'sʌmpʃn]	Annahme, Vermutung
	measurable	['meʒərəbl]	messbar, merklich
	achievable	[ə'tʃiːvəbl]	erreichbar, realisierbar
	time-bound	['taɪm baʊnd]	fristgebunden
	unbiased	[ʌn'baɪəst]	objektiv, unvoreingenommen
	to engage in sth	[ɪn'geɪdʒ ɪn]	sich mit etw beschäftigen
	forum	['fɔːrəm]	Forum
	to launch an attack at sb	[ˌlɔːntʃ ən ə'tæk ət]	einen Angriff auf jmdn starten
	grudge	[grʌdʒ]	Groll, Ärger
3	effectiveness	[ɪ'fektɪvnəs]	Effektivität, Wirksamkeit

4, Grammar summary

it is thought to	[ɪt ɪz 'θɔːt tə]	es wurde entschieden; man denkt, dass

4, Extra practice

2	primitive	['prɪmətɪv]	primitiv
3	tension	['tenʃn]	Anspannung, Spannung
	nationwide	[ˌneɪʃn'waɪd]	landesweit
4	power supply	['paʊə səplaɪ]	Elektrizitätsversorgung, Stromversorgung
5	limited access	[lɪmɪtɪd 'æksəs]	beschränkter Zugang
	workflow	['wɜːkfləʊ]	Arbeitsablauf
7	to adjourn	[ə'dʒɜːn]	vertagen, unterbrechen

Ⓐ1.23

Differentiating rejections

I'm not sure this is going to work.	Ich bin nicht sicher, ob das funktionieren wird.
That's interesting.	Das ist interessant.
I'm afraid that's out of the question.	Das kommt leider nicht infrage.
No way!	Niemals!
How can we make this work for both of us then?	Wie können wir das für uns beide vorteilhaft gestalten?

CS	dissatisfaction	[ˌdɪsˌsætɪsˈfækʃn]	Unzufriedenheit
	to tune into sth	[ˌtjuːn ˈɪntə]	sich auf etw einstellen; sich in etw hineinhören/hineinversetzen
	mildly	[ˈmaɪldli]	ein wenig, etwas
	disapproval	[ˌdɪsəˈpruːvl]	Missbilligung
	spectrum	[ˈspektrəm]	Spektrum
	refusal	[rɪˈfjuːzl]	Ablehnung, Absage, Verweigerung
	That's out of the question.	[ðæts ˌaʊt əv ðə ˈkwestʃn]	Das kommt nicht in Frage.
	brutal	[ˈbruːtl]	brutal, knallhart
	brush-off	[ˈbrʌʃ ɒf]	Absage
	No way!	[ˌnəʊ ˈweɪ]	Auf keinen Fall!
	rejection	[rɪˈdʒekʃn]	Ablehnung, Zurückweisung
	stepping stone	[ˈstepɪŋ stəʊn]	Trittstein, Sprungbrett
	to serve as a stepping stone	[ˌsɜːv əz ə ˈstepɪŋ stəʊn]	als Brücke dienen
	to differentiate	[ˌdɪfəˈrenʃieɪt]	differenzieren, unterscheiden

Business file 2 – A team meeting

2	pushy	[ˈpʊʃi]	ehrgeizig, fordernd
	diplomatic	[ˌdɪpləˈmætɪk]	diplomatisch
	wishy-washy *(coll.)*	[ˈwɪʃi wɒʃi]	vage, wischi-waschi
	to mess up	[ˌmes ˈʌp]	vermasseln, verpatzen
	to take ages	[ˌteɪk ˈeɪdʒəs]	eine Ewigkeit dauern
5	accuracy	[ˈækjərəsi]	Genauigkeit
	angle	[ˈæŋgl]	Blickwinkel, Perspektive

A team meeting

Opening / Closing a meeting

Good morning/afternoon, everyone.	Guten Morgen/Tag zusammen.
It's great you could all make it.	Toll, dass Sie es alle einrichten konnten.
OK, thanks a lot everyone. Let's finish for today.	O.k., vielen Dank an alle. Lassen Sie uns für heute aufhören.
I feel we've been really productive today.	Ich finde, wir waren heute sehr produktiv.

Referring to the agenda

The purpose of today's meeting ...	Der Zweck des heutigen Treffens ...
Our main aim today is to ...	Unser Hauptziel heute ist ...
Would anyone like to add anything to the agenda?	Möchte jemand etwas auf der Tagesordnung ergänzen?
Let's take the first item on the agenda.	Kommen wir zum ersten Punkt auf der Tagesordnung.

Opinions I

What do you think / How do you feel about that?	Was denken Sie / Wie finden Sie ...?
I'm sure/positive/convinced that ...	Ich bin sicher/überzeugt, dass ...
I think/believe/feel that we should ...	Ich denke/finde, dass wir ... sollten
The way I see it, we need to ...	So, wie ich das sehe, müssen wir ...

Agreeing and disagreeing II

That's right. / That's a good idea.	Das ist richtig / Das ist eine gute Idee.
Definitely. /Absolutely. / I totally agree with you.	Definitiv. / Absolut. / Ich stimme Ihnen voll und ganz zu.
I see what you mean, but what about ...?	Ich verstehe, was Sie meinen, aber was ist mit ...?
Why not look at it from another angle?	Wie wäre es, wenn wir das ganze aus einem anderen Blickwinkel betrachten?
I'm sorry you feel like that. What if we ...?	Es tut mir leid, dass Sie das so empfinden/ sehen. Wie wäre es, wenn wir ...?

Reaching a decision

Let me just summarize the main points.	Lassen Sie mich die wichtigsten Punkte zusammenfassen.
Are we in agreement on that?	Können wir uns darauf einigen?
Can I just have a show of hands?	Könnten Sie mir kurz ein Handzeichen geben?

5A, Doing the groundwork

▶ to get a message across	[get ə ˌmesɪdʒ əˈkrɒs]	eine Aussage vermitteln
to interact	[ˌɪntərˈækt]	miteinander umgehen

1	appliance	[ə'plaɪəns]	Gerät
1.24	ties	[taɪz]	Verbindungen, Beziehungen
	groundwork	['graʊndwɜːk]	Vorarbeit
	to **rely on** sth	[rɪ'laɪ ɒn]	auf etw vertrauen
	extension cord	[ɪk'stenʃn kɔːd]	Verlängerungskabel
	adaptor plug	[ə'dæptə plʌg]	Adapterstecker
	to **run out of** sth	[rʌn 'aʊt əv]	etw nicht mehr haben
	seating	['siːtɪŋ]	Platz, Sitzfläche
	hard copy	[ˌhɑːd 'kɒpi]	Ausdruck
	to rehearse	[rɪ'hɜːs]	proben, sich leise vorsagen
	hook	[hʊk]	Aufhänger
	to **grab** sb's **attention**	[græb ə'tenʃn]	jmds Aufmerksamkeit auf sich ziehen
	to accomplish	[ə'kʌmplɪʃ]	erreichen
	to **hook up to** sth	[ˌhʊk 'ʌp tə]	an etw angeschlossen sein
	mood	[muːd]	Stimmung, Laune
	evidence	['evɪdəns]	Beweis
	pace	[peɪs]	Tempo, Geschwindigkeit

Doing the groundwork for a presentation

Have you ...	Haben Sie ...
... made emergency backups?	... eine Sicherungskopie gemacht?
... researched the audience yet?	... sich die Zuhörer genauer angeschaut?
... made sure there's sufficient seating?	... sichergestellt, dass ausreichend Sitzplätze vorhanden sind?
... practised a few times beforehand?	... vorher ein paar Mal geübt?
Will your laptop hook up to the data projector?	Kann Ihr Laptop an den Beamer angeschlossen werden?
Make sure your laptop is not running out of power halfway through the talk.	Stellen Sie sicher, dass der Akku Ihres Laptops nicht mitten im Vortrag leer ist.

3	bullet point	['bʊlɪt pɔɪnt]	Aufzählungszeichen
	rough	[rʌf]	grob
	outline	['aʊtlaɪn]	Übersicht
	unreadable	[ʌn'riːdəbl]	nicht lesbar, schwer zu lesen

Giving advice

If I were you, / If I were in your shoes, I'd ...	An Ihrer Stelle würde ich ...
It might be a good idea if you ...	Vielleicht wäre es eine gute Idee, wenn Sie ...
Why don't you talk to him? – Good point, I'll do that.	Warum sprechen Sie nicht mit ihm? – Das ist eine gute Idee, das werde ich machen.
Whatever you do, don't forget ... – OK, got that.	Was auch immer Sie machen, vergessen Sie nicht ... – O.k., verstanden.
You might want to ... / I think you should ...	Vielleicht sollten Sie ...
Have you thought about it?	Haben Sie darüber nachgedacht?

5	circumstances	['sɜːkəmstənsɪz]	Umstände, Verhältnisse
1.25	way off	[ˌweɪ 'ɒf]	weit weg
1.26	invisible	[ɪn'vɪzəbl]	unsichtbar
	to walk up to sb	[ˌwɔːk 'ʌp tə]	auf jmdn zugehen
	frown	[fraʊn]	Stirnrunzeln
	to bother	['bɒðə]	sich kümmern
	to turn up	[ˌtɜːn 'ʌp]	auftauchen, erscheinen
8	mic = microphone	[mɪk]	Mikrofon

5B, Off to a good start

1	franchiser	['fræntʃaɪzə]	Lizenzgeber/in
	franchisee	[ˌfræntʃaɪ'ziː]	Lizenznehmer/in
	guidance	['gaɪdns]	Anleitung, Beratung
	in return for	[ɪn rɪ'tɜːn fə]	als Gegenleistung für
	household electrical goods	[haʊshəʊld ɪ'lektrɪkl gʊdz]	elektrische Haushaltsgeräte
2	to wrap up sth (coll.)	[ˌræp 'ʌp]	etw abschließen/beenden
	to hand over	[ˌhænd 'əʊvə]	weiterreichen, übergeben
	to recap	['riːkæp]	rekapitulieren, zusammenfassen
	to touch on	['tʌtʃ ɒn]	kurz berühren, streifen

How was your presentation?

Under the circumstances, it went much better than expected.	Unter diesen Umständen lief es besser als gedacht.
I got my main points across.	Ich konnte die wesentlichen Aspekte rüberbringen.
The timing couldn't have been worse.	Das Timing hätte nicht schlechter sein können.
I made the afternoon session into more of a workshop.	Ich habe den Teil am Nachmittag zu einer Art Workshop umgestaltet.
I should have made more of an effort.	Ich hätte mir mehr Mühe geben sollen.
The presentation was really bad and to make things worse, …	Die Präsentation war wirklich schlecht und als ob das nicht schlimm genug gewesen wäre …
Hardly anyone bothered to turn up.	Kaum jemand ist erschienen.

3	vast	[vɑːst]	riesig
1.28	to consist of	[kən'sɪst əv]	bestehen aus
	source	[sɔːs]	Quelle
	hot spot	['hɒt spɒt]	interessanter Ort
	by far	[ˌbaɪ 'fɑː]	bei weitem
	entry mode	['entri məʊd]	Eintrittsstrategie für den Markt
	venture	['ventʃə]	Unternehmung, Vorhaben
	to utilize	['juːtəlaɪz]	verwenden, nutzen
	to last	[lɑːst]	dauern
	economic	[ˌiːkə'nɒmɪk]	wirtschaftlich
4	in the long run	[ɪn ðə 'lɒŋ rʌn]	auf lange Sicht, auf die Dauer
	to adopt	[ə'dɒpt]	annehmen, übernehmen

carbon footprint	[ˌkɑːbən ˈfʊtprɪnt]	CO_2-Bilanz
to take questions	[ˌteɪk ˈkwestʃns]	Fragen beantworten
5 principle	[ˈprɪnsɪpl]	Prinzip
🔊1.29 to conclude sth from sth	[kənˈkluːd frəm]	etw aus etw schließen, ableiten
persistent	[pəˈsɪstənt]	beharrlich, hartnäckig
thriving	[ˈθraɪvɪŋ]	blühend, florierend
swift	[swɪft]	schnell, rasch
real time	[ˌrɪəl ˈtaɪm]	Echtzeit

Starting a presentation

I'm going to talk about …	Ich werde über … reden.
The talk will take 15 minutes.	Der Vortrag wird 15 Minuten dauern.
I'll take questions at the end.	Auf Fragen werde ich am Ende eingehen.
The subject of today's presentation is …	Das Thema der heutigen Präsentation ist …
First of all, I'd like to … Then I'll move on to …	Zunächst/Zuerst würde ich gerne … Danach werde ich mit … weitermachen.
And finally, I'll …	Schließlich werde ich …
After that, I'll hand over to …	Danach übergebe ich das Wort an …
If nobody has any questions, I'll start.	Wenn niemand Fragen hat, würde ich jetzt beginnen.

8 to signpost	[ˈsaɪnpəʊst]	schildern, ausschildern
anecdote	[ˈænɪkdəʊt]	Anekdote, persönlicher Bericht
thoughtful	[ˈθɔːtfl]	gut durchdacht, wohl überlegt

Ending a presentation

That was a brief overview of …	Das war ein kurzer Überblick über …
I hope that's given you some idea of …	Ich hoffe, das hat Ihnen einen Eindruck von … gegeben.
To conclude, let me just review the main points. Firstly / Secondly / Finally …	Lassen Sie mich abschließend die wichtigsten Punkte nochmal zusammenfassen. Erstens / Zweitens / Schließlich …
I showed …	Ich habe gezeigt …
That just about wraps things up.	Das ist im Großen und Ganzen alles.
That brings me to the end of my presentation today.	Das bringt mich zum Ende meiner heutigen Präsentation.
I apologize for going 15 minutes over the time.	Es tut mir leid, dass ich 15 Minuten überzogen habe.
I will now be happy to answer more of your questions.	Ich beantworte jetzt gerne Ihre Fragen.

9	delegation	[ˌdelɪ'ɡeɪʃn]	Delegation, Abordnung
	drama	['drɑːmə]	Dramatik, Schauspiel
	props	[prɒps]	Requisiten, *hier:* Gegenstand
	nail	[neɪl]	Nagel
	to stick up	[ˌstɪk 'ʌp]	in die Höhe stehen, herausstehen
	to hit	[hɪt]	schlagen
	hammer	['hæmə]	Hammer
	to pace	[peɪs]	das Tempo bestimmen

5C, Meet Derek Sivers

▶	entrepreneur	[ˌɒntrəprə'nɜː]	Unternehmer/in
	to imitate	['ɪmɪteɪt]	imitieren, nachahmen
	to go with the flow	[ˌɡəʊ wɪð ðə 'fləʊ]	mit dem Strom schwimmen
	path	[pɑːθ]	Weg, Pfad
1	to start	[stɑːt]	gründen, aufmachen
	charity	['tʃærəti]	Wohltätigkeits-
	programmer	['prəʊɡræmə]	Programmierer/in
	avid	['ævɪd]	begeistert, leidenschaftlich
	to go on to do sth	[ɡəʊ ˌɒn tə 'du]	dann etw tun
	proceeds	['prəʊsiːdz]	Erlös
	mansion	['mænʃn]	Villa, herrschaftlicher Wohnsitz
	billionaire	[ˌbɪljə'neə]	Milliardär/in
	guy	[ɡaɪ]	Typ, Kerl
	excess	[ɪk'ses]	Exzess, Übermaß
	charitable	['tʃærətəbl]	gemeinnützig, wohltätig
	trust	[trʌst]	Stiftung
	musician	[mju'zɪʃn]	Musiker/in
	to die	[daɪ]	sterben
	alive	[ə'laɪv]	am Leben, lebendig
	to pay out	[ˌpeɪ 'aʊt]	auszahlen
2	disinterested	[dɪs'ɪntrəstɪd]	desinteressiert
	ambition	[æm'bɪʃn]	Ambition, Ehrgeiz
3	identity	[aɪ'dentəti]	Identität
	psychology	[saɪ'kɒlədʒi]	Psychologie
	to prove	[pruːv]	beweisen
	to acknowledge	[ək'nɒlɪdʒ]	anerkennen, bestätigen
	to trick	[trɪk]	täuschen, hereinlegen
	to trick sb into sth	[ˌtrɪk 'ɪntə]	jmdn mit einem Trick zu etw bringen
	conventional	[kən'venʃnl]	herkömmlich, üblich
	wisdom	['wɪzdəm]	Weisheit
	conventional wisdom	[kənvenʃnl 'wɪzdəm]	herrschende Meinung
	proof	[pruːf]	Beweis
	substitution	[ˌsʌbstɪ'tjuːʃn]	Ersatz
	to keep your mouth shut *(coll.)*	[kiːp jɔː 'maʊθ ʃʌt]	den Mund halten
	to quit	[kwɪt]	aufhören
	temptation	[temp'teɪʃn]	Versuchung, Verlockung
	gratification	[ˌɡrætɪfɪ'keɪʃn]	Befriedigung

acknowledgement	[ək'nɒlɪdʒmənt]	Anerkennung
to **mistake** sth **for** sth	[mɪ'steɪk fə]	etw für etw halten, etw mit etw verwechseln
to **kick** one's **ass** (coll.)	[kɪk wʌnz 'æs]	jmdm in den Hintern treten
to **tempt** sb	[tempt]	in Versuchung führen
4 **build up**	['bɪld ʌp]	Aufbau
visual	['vɪʒuəl]	Anschauungsmaterial

5, Grammar summary

| to **bore** | [bɔː] | langweilen |

5, Extra practice

2 **prompt**	[prɒmpt]	Stichwort
4 **robotics**	[rəʊ'bɒtɪks]	Robotertechnik, Robotik
namely	['neɪmli]	nämlich, und zwar
6 **peak**	[piːk]	Höhepunkt
1.31 **fatigue**	[fə'tiːg]	Ermüdung
alert	[ə'lɜːt]	aufmerksam, munter
1.32 to **apply for**	[ə'plaɪ fə]	beantragen
permit	['pɜːmɪt]	Genehmigung, Erlaubnis
7 to **keep track of** sth	[ˌkiːp 'træk əv]	den Überblick über etw behalten
9 to **lose** your **cool** (coll.)	[ˌluːz jɔː 'kuːl]	die Fassung verlieren, sich aus der Ruhe bringen lassen
CS to **pitch**	[pɪtʃ]	hier: vortragen
idiomatic	[ˌɪdiə'mætɪk]	idiomatisch
turn of phrase	[ˌtɜːn əv 'freɪz]	Ausdrucksweise
to **shoot** yourself **in the foot** (coll.)	[ˌʃuːt jɔːself ɪn ðə 'fʊt]	ein Eigentor schießen
to **overwhelm**	[ˌəʊvə'welm]	überwältigen, überschütten
huge	[hjuːdʒ]	riesig, Riesen-
succinct	[sək'sɪŋkt]	kurz und treffend, prägnant
to **get down to** the **nitty-gritty** (coll.)	[get ˌdaʊn tə ðə ˌnɪti 'grɪti]	zur Sache kommen

Keeping things simple

Don't pitch your presentation at a high level.	Setzen Sie Ihre Präsentation nicht auf einem (zu) hohen Niveau an.
Don't be tempted to slip in …	Versuchen Sie nicht … einzuwerfen.
You may end up shooting yourself in the foot. (coll.)	Damit könnten Sie sich ins eigene Fleisch schneiden.
Aim for a very basic and clear style of expression.	Bemühen Sie sich um eine klare und deutliche Ausdrucksweise.
Give a succinct overview of …	Geben Sie einen kurzen Überblick über …
Get down to the nitty-gritty. (coll.)	Kommen Sie zur Sache.
Maintain good eye contact throughout.	Halten Sie durchgängig Augenkontakt.

6A, Picture this

►	to quote	[kwəʊt]	zitieren
1	concrete	['kɒŋkriːt]	Beton
	cement	[sɪ'mənt]	Zement
	to aim at sth	[eɪm ət]	etw beabsichtigen, etw anstreben
	insight	['ɪnsaɪt]	Einblick
	strategic	[strə'tiːdʒɪk]	strategisch
	GTKY = Getting to know you	[dʒi: tiː keɪ 'waɪ]	Kennenlern-
2	bar chart	['bɑː tʃɑːt]	Stabdiagramm, Balkendiagramm
	flow chart	['fləʊ tʃɑːt]	Flussdiagramm
3	composite	['kɒmpəzɪt]	zusammengesetzt
	aggregate	['ægrɪgət]	Betonzuschlag; Summe, Gesamtwert
	gravel	['grævl]	Kies
	crushed stone	['krʌʃd stəʊn]	Schotter
	limestone	['laɪmstəʊn]	Kalkstein
	mineral	['mɪnərəl]	Mineral
	to absorb	[əb'sɔːb]	aufnehmen
	to intend to	[ɪn'tend tə]	beabsichtigen, vorhaben
	ready-mix concrete	[ˌredi mɪks 'kɒŋkriːt]	Fertigbeton
	to privatize	['praɪvətaɪz]	privatisieren
	trillion	['trɪljən]	Billion
4	roughly	['rʌfli]	ungefähr, grob
⊚²2.2	to put into perspective	[ˌpʊt ɪntə pə'spektɪv]	relativieren
	to soar	[sɔː]	in die Höhe schnellen, ansteigen
	to plummet	['plʌmɪt]	stürzen, absacken
	sparse	[spɑːs]	spärlich
	sparsly populated	[spɑːsli 'pɒpjuleɪtɪd]	dünn besiedelt
	inhabitant	[ɪn'hæbɪtənt]	Einwohner/in
	ton	[tʌn]	Tonne
	state-owned	['steɪt əʊnd]	staatlich, Staats-
	deregulation	[ˌdiːˌregju'leɪʃn]	Deregulierung
	market economy	[mɑːkɪt ɪ'kɒnəmi]	Marktwirtschaft
	relative	['relətɪv]	verhältnismäßig, relativ
	lack	[læk]	Mangel
	somewhat	['sʌmwɒt]	etwas, ziemlich
	to regain	[rɪ'geɪn]	wiedergewinnen
	consumption	[kən'sʌmpʃn]	Verbrauch, Konsum
	excited	[ɪk'saɪtɪd]	begeistert
	to set a goal	[ˌset ə 'gəʊl]	ein Ziel setzen
6	versus	['vɜːsəs]	gegen, gegenüber
7	to guide	[gaɪd]	führen, leiten

Structuring a presentation

As you can see here, …	Wie Sie hier sehen können, …
The next slide shows … / Let's turn to…	Die nächste Folie zeigt … / Wenden wir uns … zu.
To illustrate this, may I draw your attention to …	Um dies zu veranschaulichen, würde ich Ihre Aufmerksamkeit gerne auf … lenken.
As I mentioned/said before, …	Wie ich zuvor bereits erwähnt/gesagt habe, …
This might surprise you, but …	Dies könnte Sie überraschen, aber …
I want to keep you in suspense a little longer.	Ich möchte Sie noch ein bisschen auf die Folter spannen.

 2.3

cautious	['kɔːʃəs]	vorsichtig
to lay off	[ˌleɪ 'ɒf]	entlassen
whereas	[ˌweər'æz]	während, dagegen
to map out	[ˌmæp 'aʊt]	festlegen, vorlegen, aufzeigen
9 recruit	[rɪ'kruːt]	Neuzugang
to interpret	[ɪn'tɜːprɪt]	deuten, interpretieren

6B, The Q & A session

○	worst case scenario	[ˌwɜːst keɪs sə'nɑːriəʊ]	der schlimmste Fall, größter anzunehmender Unfall - GAU
	flash drive	['flæʃ draɪv]	USB-Stick
1	to steal	[stiːl]	stehlen
2	rich	[rɪtʃ]	reichhaltig, reich
	hesitant	['hezɪtənt]	zögernd, zaghaft
	to double	['dʌbl]	(sich) verdoppeln
	to triple	['trɪpl]	verdreifachen
3	repeated	[rɪ'piːtɪd]	wiederholt
	mining consultant	['maɪnɪŋ kənsʌltənt]	Fachberater/in für den Bergbau
4	to change for the better	[ˌtʃeɪndʒ fə ðə 'betə]	sich zum Besseren verändern
	to change for the worse	[ˌtʃeɪndʒ fə ðə 'wɜːs]	sich zum Schlechteren verändern
	standard of living	[ˌstændəd əv 'lɪvɪŋ]	Lebensstandard
	confident	['kɒnfɪdənt]	selbstbewusst, selbstsicher
	command	[kə'mɑːnd]	Beherrschung, Beherrschen
5	row	[rəʊ]	Reihe
	bottleneck	['bɒtlnek]	Engpass, Flaschenhals
	bottleneck point	['bɒtlnek pɔɪnt]	Engpass, Engstelle
	to smuggle	['smʌgl]	schmuggeln
	to procure	[prə'kjʊə]	beschaffen
	to slump	[slʌmp]	fallen, sinken
	to dip	[dɪp]	tauchen, sinken
	to sink	[sɪŋk]	sinken, absinken
6	chamber of commerce	[ˌtʃeɪmbər əv 'kɒmɜːs]	Handelskammer
2.4 border	['bɔːdə]	Grenze
	tax	[tæks]	Steuer
	to exceed	[ɪk'siːd]	überschreiten, übertreffen

supply	[sə'plaɪ]	*hier:* Angebot, Vorrat
smuggling	['smʌglɪŋ]	Schmuggel, Schmuggeln
irregularity	[ɪˌregjə'lærəti]	Regelwidrigkeit, Verstoß
building	['bɪldɪŋ]	Bau
a great deal	[ə ˌgreɪt 'diːl]	eine Menge, viel
to shut down	[ˌʃʌt 'daʊn]	schließen
to consolidate	[kən'sɒlɪdeɪt]	*Unternehmen etc.:* zusammenlegen
to address sth to sb	[ə'dres tə]	etw an jmdn richten

7	patient	['peɪʃnt]	geduldig
8	to differ	['dɪfə]	unterscheiden, sich unterscheiden
	dependent on	[dɪ'pendənt ɒn]	abhängig
9	to deserve	[dɪ'zɜːv]	verdienen, wert sein
	to breed	[briːd]	hervorrufen, brüten
	to memorize	['meməraɪz]	auswendig lernen, sich einprägen

Handling questions

I see what you mean. Can we come back to that later?	Ich verstehe, was Sie meinen. Können wir darauf später zurückkommen?
Sorry, I didn't express that clearly. What I meant to say was …	Tut mir leid, da habe ich mich nicht klar genug ausgedrückt. Was ich sagen wollte, war …
Well, in other words …	Nun, mit anderen Worten …
I'm afraid I can't give you a full answer to your question at this state, but …	Leider kann ich Ihnen zum jetzigen Zeitpunkt Ihre Frage nicht vollständig beantworten, aber …
Sorry, I don't know the answer to that but I'll find out.	Tut mir leid, darauf weiß ich keine Antwort, aber ich werde mich erkundigen.
Does that answer your question?	Beantwortet das Ihre Frage?
Just bear with me for a moment while I check …	Bitte gedulden Sie sich einen Moment während ich … anschaue.

6C, Lost and found

●	ship	[ʃɪp]	Schiff
	to recall	[rɪ'kɔːl]	*Produkt:* zurückrufen
1	measure	['meʒə]	Maß, Maßstab
	in place	[ɪn 'pleɪs]	etabliert
	to go missing	[gəʊ 'mɪsɪŋ]	verloren gehen
	insecurity	[ˌɪnsɪ'kjʊərəti]	Unsicherheit
	to rush	[rʌʃ]	eilen, hetzen
	business traveler	['bɪznəs trævələ]	Geschäftsreisende/r
	sensitive	['sensətɪv]	empfindlich, sensibel
	confidential	[ˌkɒnfɪ'denʃl]	vertraulich, persönlich
	to put at risk	[pʊt ət 'rɪsk]	einem Risiko aussetzen, gefährden
	noticeable	['nəʊtɪsəbl]	deutlich, auffällig
	to misplace	[ˌmɪs'pleɪs]	verlegen

lost and found department	[ˌlɒst ən ˈfaʊnd]	Fundbüro
to reclaim	[rɪˈkleɪm]	zurückverlangen, abholen
unclaimed	[ˌʌnˈkleɪmd]	herrenlos, nicht abgeholt
to dispose of sth	[dɪˈspəʊz əv]	sich einer Sache entledigen
accessible	[əkˈsesəbl]	zugänglich
recovery	[rɪˈkʌveri]	Wiederbeschaffung, Wiedererlangung
comparable	[ˈkɒmpərəbl]	vergleichbar
security checkpoint	[sɪˈkjʊərəti tʃekpɔɪnt]	Sicherheitskontrolle
EMEA = Europe, Middle East, Africa	[iː em iː ˈeɪ]	Wirtschaftsraum Europa, Naher Osten, Afrika
stupid	[ˈstjuːpɪd]	dumm, blöd
to think ahead	[ˌθɪŋk əˈhed]	vorausdenken, vorausplanen
mental	[ˈmentl]	geistig
to screen	[skriːn]	untersuchen, überprüfen
encryption	[ɪnˈkrɪpʃn]	Verschlüsselung
to back up sth	[ˌbæk ˈʌp]	eine Sicherheitskopie von etw anlegen; *hier:* etw erläutern, etw belegen
owner	[ˈəʊnə]	Besitzer/in
3 to destroy	[dɪˈstrɔɪ]	zerstören, vernichten
4 to retrieve	[rɪˈtriːv]	zurückholen
⏻ 2.5 to recover	[rɪˈkʌvə]	wiedererlangen, zurückbekommen, wiederherstellen
nightmare	[ˈnaɪtmeə]	Albtraum
on top	[ɒn ˈtɒp]	zusätzlich
pouring rain	[ˌpɔːrɪŋ ˈreɪn]	strömender Regen
soaked	[səʊkt]	durchnässt
to make the plane	[ˌmeɪk ðə ˈpleɪn]	den Flieger bekommen
to exhale	[eksˈheɪl]	durchatmen, ausatmen
to hit sb *(coll.)*	[hɪt]	jmdm aufgehen/einfallen
back seat	[ˌbæk ˈsiːt]	Rücksitz, Rückbank
to register	[ˈredʒɪstə]	registrieren
sticker	[ˈstɪkə]	Aufkleber
subscription fee	[səbˈskrɪpʃn fiː]	Mitgliedsbeitrag
to track down	[ˌtræk ˈdaʊn]	ausfindig machen, finden
to pre-install	[ˌpriː ˈɪnstɔːl]	vorinstallieren
to reveal	[rɪˈviːl]	erkennen lassen, zeigen
remotely	[rɪˈməʊtli]	*hier:* fern-, von Ferne
in-built	[ˈɪnbɪlt]	eingebaut
thief	[θiːf]	Dieb/in
to raise	[reɪz]	heben, erhöhen
4 outside	[ˌaʊtˈsaɪd]	außerhalb
theft	[θeft]	Diebstahl
6 to shock	[ʃɒk]	schocken, erschüttern

6, Grammar summary

profitable	[ˈprɒfɪtəbl]	gewinnbringend, einträglich

6, Extra practice

1	considerable	[kən'sɪdərəbl]	erheblich, beträchtlich
3	dense	[dens]	dicht
	comprehensive	[ˌkɒmprɪ'hensɪv]	umfassend, erschöpfend
4	modifier	['mɒdɪfaɪə]	Modifikator
	Q&A = question and answer	[ˌkjuː ənd 'eɪ]	Frage und Antwort
5	on my feet	[ɒn maɪ 'fiːt]	aus dem Stegreif, in schlagfertiger Art
6	organigram	[ɔː'gænɪgræm]	Organigramm
	likewise	['laɪkwaɪz]	ebenso, gleichfalls
8 ◖◗2.6	to carry a risk	[ˌkeri ə 'rɪsk]	ein Risiko bergen, risikobehaftet sein
9	to stagnate	[stæg'neɪt]	stagnieren
CS	widely	['waɪdli]	sehr, erheblich
	to display	[dɪ'spleɪ]	zeigen
	to frown	[fraʊn]	die Stirn runzeln
	reserved	[rɪ'zɜːvd]	zurückhaltend, reserviert
	poker-faced	['pəʊkəfeɪsd]	mit unbewegter Miene
	to confront sb with sth	[kən'frʌnt wɪð]	jmdn mit etw konfrontieren
	stare	[steə]	Starren
	deep	[diːp]	tief
	breath	[breθ]	Atem, Atemzug
	to take in	[ˌteɪk 'ɪn]	begreifen
	to invite sth	[ɪn'vaɪt]	etw erbitten
	participation	[pɑːˌtɪsɪ'peɪʃn]	Teilnahme, Beteiligung
	inappropriate	[ˌɪnə'prəʊpriət]	unangemessen, unpassend
	reluctant	[rɪ'lʌktənt]	zögerlich

Getting your message across

Audiences might …
… display their emotions openly in public.
… be reserved, even poker-faced.

… confront you with blank stares.
Invite questions during the talk.

Zuhörer könnten …
… ihre Gefühle offen zeigen.
… reserviert sein, sogar eine unbewegte Miene haben.
… mit leerem Blick zurückstarren.
Ermutigen Sie (Ihr Publikum) während des Vortrags, Fragen zu stellen.

Business file 3 – A presentation

1	action items	['ækʃn aɪtəms]	offene Punkte, umzusetzende Maßnahmen
	to finish up	[ˌfɪnɪʃ 'ʌp]	enden
◖◗2.7	auction	['ɔːkʃn]	Auktion
	reverse auction	[rɪˌvɜːs 'ɔːkʃn]	Ausschreibung, Auftragsauktion
	to bid	[bɪd]	bieten, ein Angebot machen
	fine	[faɪn]	Geldstrafe, Geldbuße

tolerance	['tɒlərəns]	Toleranz, Abweichung
circuit	['sɜːkɪt]	Stromkreis
printed circuit board	[ˌprɪntəd 'sɜːkɪt bɔːd]	Leiterplatte, Platine
to starve	[stɑːv]	hungern, verhungern
to be starving (coll.)	[bi 'stɑːvɪŋ]	einen Wahnsinnshunger haben

	lateness	['leɪtnəs]	Verspätung
2	outcome	['aʊtkʌm]	Ergebnis, Resultat
	course of action	[ˌkɔːs əv 'ækʃn]	Vorgehen, Handlungsschritt
	regulatory	['reɡjələtəri]	Aufsichts-
	regulatory board	[ˌreɡjələtəri 'bɔːd]	Aufsichtsrat, Aufsichtsgremium
	compliance	[kəm'plaɪəns]	Befolgung, Einhaltung
3	outgoing shipment	['aʊtɡəʊɪŋ ʃɪpmənt]	Warenversand
	to compete	[kəm'piːt]	konkurrieren, kämpfen
	to fine	[faɪn]	zu einer Geldstrafe verurteilen
	to blacklist	['blæklɪst]	auf die schwarze Liste setzen
	liable	['laɪəbl]	haftbar
	assembly	[ə'sembli]	Montage
	to certify	['sɜːtɪfaɪ]	zertifizieren, bescheinigen
	in regard to	[ɪn rɪ'ɡɑːd tə]	in Bezug auf
	to investigate	[ɪn'vestɪɡeɪt]	ermitteln, untersuchen
4	basic	['beɪsɪk]	einfach, grundlegend

7A, Finding a new business partner

	to struggle	['strʌɡl]	sich schwertun, sich abmühen
1	to struggle	['strʌɡl]	sich schwertun, sich abmühen
	coating	['kəʊtɪŋ]	Beschichtung
	to go the extra mile	[ˌɡəʊ ði 'ekstrə maɪl]	keine Mühen scheuen
	speciality ingredients	[speʃiˌæləti ɪn'ɡriːdiənts]	Spezialrohstoffe
	basic chemical	[ˌbeɪsɪk 'kemɪkl]	Grundchemikalie, chemischer Grundstoff
	phosphoric acid	[fɒsˌfɒrɪk 'æsɪd]	Phosphorsäure
	fungal	['fʌnɡl]	Pilz-
	biocide	['baɪəʊsaɪd]	Biozid, Pestizid
2	to approach sb	[ə'prəʊtʃ]	an jmdn herantreten
2.8	to read up on sth	[ˌriːd 'ʌp ɒn]	sich über etw informieren, etw recherchieren
	compound	['kɒmpaʊnd]	Mischung, Verbindung
	biocidal	[baɪəʊ'saɪdl]	biozid
	flooring	['flɔːrɪŋ]	Belag, Bodenbelag
	kitchen top	[ˌkɪtʃn 'tɒp]	Küchenarbeitsplatte
	to consider	[kən'sɪdə]	berücksichtigen, erwägen, in Betracht ziehen
	to stand	[stænd]	stehen, hoch sein
	margin	['mɑːdʒɪn]	Spielraum
	profit margin	['prɒfɪt mɑːdʒɪn]	Gewinnspanne
	to be to do sth	[ˌbi tə 'duː]	etw tun sollen
	compromise	['kɒmprəmaɪz]	Kompromiss
	to gain access	[ˌɡeɪn 'ækses]	Zugang erhalten

objection	[əb'dʒekʃn]	Einwand
pricing	['praɪsɪŋ]	Preis
to mix	[mɪks]	mischen
to reconsider	[ˌriːkən'sɪdə]	noch einmal überdenken
to work sth out	[ˌwɜːk 'aut]	sich etw ausdenken
in addition	[ɪn ə'dɪʃn]	zusätzlich

	ideally	[aɪ'diːəli]	idealerweise
5	must-have	[ˌmʌst 'hæv]	ein Muss
	bottom line	[ˌbɒtəm 'laɪn]	Fazit, das Entscheidende
	concession	[kən'seʃn]	Zugeständnis
	deadlock	['dedlɒk]	festgefahrene Situation
	to haggle	['hægl]	feilschen
	trade-off	['treɪdɒf]	Kompromiss, Ausgleich
	win-win	[ˌwɪn'wɪn]	gewinnbringend für beide Seiten
	to compromise	['kɒmprəmaɪz]	sich einigen, einen Kompromiss schließen
	company car	[ˌkʌmpəni 'kɑː]	Geschäftswagen
	salary increase	[ˌsæləri 'ɪnkriːs]	Lohnerhöhung
	collaboration	[kə'læbə'reɪʃn]	Zusammenarbeit
6	to buy up	[ˌbaɪ 'ʌp]	aufkaufen

7	to leave open	[ˌliːv 'əupən]	offenlassen, offenhalten
2.9	sceptical	['skeptɪkl]	skeptisch
	in light of	[ɪn 'laɪt əv]	angesichts
	to hint	[hɪnt]	andeuten

10	to relocate	[ˌriːləu'keɪt]	umsiedeln, den Standort verlegen

Considering possibilities

Might you consider doing things this way?	Könnten Sie sich vorstellen, das so zu machen?
Would you be open to this possibility?	Wären Sie dieser Möglichkeit gegenüber offen?
Mightn't it be better to …?	Wäre es nicht besser …?
I'm afraid we can't consider that possibility at the moment.	Leider können wir diese Möglichkeit momentan nicht in Betracht ziehen.
If I did that, would I have to do anything else in addition?	Was käme darüber hinaus auf mich zu, wenn ich zustimme / mich darauf einlasse?
If you were to consider doing that …	Wenn Sie das in Betracht ziehen könnten …

7B, Making concessions

	dance	[dɑːns]	Tanz
	battle	['bætl]	Kampf
1	insufficient	[ˌɪnsə'fɪʃnt]	unzureichend, nicht genug
	infrastructure	['ɪnfrəstrʌktʃə]	Infrastruktur
	commercial issues	[kəˌmɜːʃl 'ɪʃuːs]	Faktoren mit Bezug auf Handel und Vertrieb

to overlap	[ˌəʊvəˈlæp]	sich überschneiden
2 to be desperate for	[bi ˈdespərət fə]	etw dringend brauchen
narrow	[ˈnærəʊ]	schmal, beschränkt

🔊 2.10

3 That remains to be seen.	[ðæt rɪˌmeɪns tə bi ˈsiːn]	Das bleibt abzuwarten.
to doubt	[daʊt]	an-/bezweifeln, nicht trauen
to bring up	[ˌbrɪŋ ˈʌp]	ansprechen, erwähnen
-wise	[waɪz]	-mäßig, was … betrifft
with no reservation	[wɪð nəʊ ˌrezəˈveɪʃn]	ohne Vorbehalt

4 in bold	[ɪn ˈbəʊld]	fett gedruckt
to point out	[ˌpɔɪnt ˈaʊt]	betonen, hervorheben
to check up on sth	[ˌtʃek ˈʌp ɒn]	etw überprüfen
to walk away from sth	[ˌwɔːk əˈweɪ frəm]	etw aus dem Weg gehen, vor etw davonlaufen
to call attention	[tə ˌkɔːl əˈtenʃn]	Aufmerksamkeit erregen
to verify	[ˈverɪfaɪ]	überprüfen, bestätigen
6 however	[haʊˈevə]	wie … auch

🔊 2.11

to look at sth	[ˈlʊk ət]	etw in Betracht ziehen
bear in mind	[beər ɪn ˈmaɪnd]	denken Sie daran, vergessen Sie nicht
uneconomical	[ˌʌnˌiːkəˈnɒmɪkl]	unwirtschaftlich

7 clarity	[ˈklærəti]	Klarheit, Direktheit
match	[mætʃ]	Gegenstück
8 timescale	[ˈtaɪmskeɪl]	zeitlicher Rahmen
in principle	[ɪn ˈprɪnsɪpl]	im Prinzip
to play for time	[ˌpleɪ fə ˈtaɪm]	Zeit gewinnen, Zeit schinden
9 ignorance	[ˈɪgnərəns]	Ignoranz
illusion	[ɪˈluːʒn]	Illusion, Täuschung

Negotiating styles

That's my last and final offer. Take it or leave it!	Das ist wirklich mein allerletztes Angebot! Nehmen Sie es an oder lassen Sie's.
That's absolutely non-negotiable.	Das ist absolut nicht verhandelbar.
That's a definite must-have for me.	Das ist definitiv ein Muss für mich.
I'm afraid I can't make any concessions on this point.	Leider kann ich bei diesem Punkt keine Zugeständnisse machen.
I'm not sure that works for us.	Ich bin mir nicht sicher, ob das für uns in Ordnung ist.
Why should we do this?	Warum sollten wir das tun?
How could you optimize this for us?	Könnten Sie uns da entgegenkommen?
Let me put it this way: …	Lassen Sie es mich so sagen: …
I've changed my position on that issue.	Ich habe meine Haltung/Einstellung diesbezüglich geändert.
I can see that working. Do we have a deal?	Ich denke, das geht. Sind wir im Geschäft?

7C, Strategic partnerships

●	to tighten	['taɪtn]	straffen
1	parameter	[pə'ræmɪtə]	Parameter
	to set the parameters	[set ðə pə'ræmɪtəz]	den Rahmen setzen
	operational	[ˌɒpə'reɪʃənl]	betrieblich, Einsatz-, betriebsbereit
	procurement department	[prə'kjʊəmənt dɪ'pɑːtmənt]	Einkaufsabteilung
	to send out	[ˌsend 'aʊt]	verschicken
	request for proposal (RFP)	[rɪˌkwest fə prə'pəʊzl]	(komplexe) Ausschreibung
	player	['pleɪə]	Akteur/in
	tube	[tjuːb]	Rohr, Röhre
	stainless steel	[ˌsteɪnləs 'stiːl]	Edelstahl
	serial	['sɪəriəl]	Serien-, Fortsetzungs-
	long-lasting	[ˌlɒŋ'lɑːstɪŋ]	dauerhaft, anhaltend
	cooperative sourcing	[kəʊˈɒpərətɪv sɔːsɪŋ]	Einkaufskooperation
	once in a while	[ˌwʌns ɪn ə 'waɪl]	von Zeit zu Zeit
	outside	[ˌaʊt'saɪd]	hier: draußen, nach draußen
	benchmark	['bentʃmɑːk]	Maßstab
4	newborn	['njuːbɔːn]	gerade geboren
	to get in the way of	[get ɪn ðə 'weɪ əv]	in die Quere kommen

7, Grammar summary

lucrative	['luːkrətɪv]	lukrativ, einträglich
to get on	[ˌget 'ɒn]	weiterkommen, vorankommen
to bring in	[ˌbrɪŋ 'ɪn]	zum Einsatz bringen, einbringen

7, Extra practice

1	after all	[ˌɑːftər 'ɔːl]	letzten Endes, schließlich
cs	leisurely	['leʒəli]	geruhsam, gemütlich
	egalitarian	[iˌgælɪ'teəriən]	egalitär
	collaboratively	[kə'læbərətɪvli]	gemeinsam
	to stall	[stɔːl]	zum Stillstand kommen, ins Stocken geraten
	distraction	[dɪ'strækʃn]	Störung, Ablenkung
	brisk	[brɪsk]	brüsk, lebhaft

8A, Across cultures

●	to speculate	['spekjuleɪt]	spekulieren, Vermutungen anstellen
	to perceive	[pə'siːv]	wahrnehmen, annehmen
1	to play a role	[ˌpleɪ ə 'rəʊl]	eine Rolle spielen
	go-ahead	['gəʊ əhed]	grünes Licht
	bewildered	[bɪ'wɪldəd]	verwirrt, verwundert
	irritated	['ɪrɪteɪtɪd]	verärgert
2	amazed	[ə'meɪzd]	erstaunt, verwundert

	annoying	[ə'nɔɪɪŋ]	lästig, ärgerlich
	bewildering	[bɪ'wɪldərɪŋ]	verwirrend
	envious	['envɪəs]	neidisch
	fascinated	['fæsɪneɪtɪd]	fasziniert
	fascinating	['fæsɪneɪtɪŋ]	faszinierend
	furious	['fjʊərɪəs]	wütend
	infuriating	[ɪn'fjʊərieɪtɪŋ]	ärgerlich
	puzzling	['pʌzlɪŋ]	rätselhaft
	stunning	['stʌnɪŋ]	fantastisch, umwerfend
	surprised	[sə'praɪzd]	überrascht, verwundert
3	probable	['prɒbəbl]	wahrscheinlich
4	to make eye contact	[meɪk 'aɪ kɒntækt]	Blickkontakt aufnehmen
	shy	[ʃaɪ]	schüchtern, scheu
5	sarcastic	[sɑː'kæstɪk]	sarkastisch
2.12	to get through sth	[ˌget 'θruː]	etw durchhalten/durchstehen
	hat	[hæt]	Hut
	Brit *(coll.)*	[brɪt]	Brite, Britin
	to okay	[əʊ'keɪ]	genehmigen
	technical writer	[teknɪkl 'raɪtə]	technische/r Redakteur/in
	ahead of	[ə'hed ɒf]	vor, voraus
	in print	[ɪn 'prɪnt]	gedruckt

Talking about behaviours

Why doesn't she give me the go ahead to …?	Warum gibt Sie mir kein grünes Licht für …?
The boss won't okay it.	Die Chefin/Der Chef wird das nicht absegnen.
That's a bit of a puzzle.	Das ist ein bisschen verwirrend.
I don't want to …, let alone …	Ich will nicht …, geschweige denn …
They may just be testing the waters.	Sie möchten vielleicht nur die Lage ausloten.
It's important not to lose face.	Es ist wichtig, sein Gesicht zu wahren.

8	sociable	['səʊʃəbl]	gesellig
	to pass sb	[pɑːs]	an jmdm vorbeigehen
	business etiquette	['bɪznəs etɪket]	Geschäftsetikette
	to do research into sth	[du rɪ'sɜːtʃ ɪntə]	etw näher untersuchen
9	mealtime	['miːltaɪm]	Essenszeit
	to recognize	['rekəgnaɪz]	anerkennen, *hier:* einhalten
	in a social setting	[ɪn ə ˌsəʊʃl 'setɪŋ]	in Gesellschaft
	honour	['ɒnə]	Ehre
	to decline	[dɪ'klaɪn]	ablehnen
	a number of times	[ə ˌnʌmbər əv 'taɪms]	mehrfach, mehrmals
	chief	[tʃiːf]	Haupt-
	negotiator	[nɪ'gəʊʃieɪtə]	Unterhändler/in
	difficulty	['dɪfɪkəlti]	Schwierigkeit, Problem
	to translate	[træns'leɪt]	übersetzen
	with hindsight	[wɪð 'haɪndsaɪt]	im Nachhinein
	sadly	['sædli]	leider, bedauerlicherweise
10	chemistry	['kemɪstri]	Chemie

| snake | [sneɪk] | Schlange |
| to smell | [smel] | riechen |

8B, A win-win solution

▶	to improve on sth	[ɪm'prəʊv ɒn]	etw verbessern
1	closed question	[kləʊzd 'kwestʃn]	Entscheidungsfrage
3	broad	[brɔːd]	breit, ausgedehnt
	to take on	[ˌteɪk 'ɒn]	annehmen
5	self-serve buffet	[self ˌsɜːv 'bʊfeɪ]	Selbstbedienungsbuffet
🔊 2.14	post-production	[ˌpəʊstprə'dʌkʃn]	Nachbearbeitung
	editing	['edɪtɪŋ]	Schnitt, Bearbeitung
	to leave out	[ˌliːv 'aʊt]	auslassen
	storyboard	['stɔːrɪbɔːd]	Storyboard, Ablaufplan
	sneak preview	[ˌsniːk 'priːvjuː]	Vorpremiere
	to have a sneak preview	[həv ə ˌsniːk 'priːvjuː]	etw im Voraus sehen
	content	['kɒntent]	Inhalt

Open questions and requests

When do you think you could …?	Wann könnten Sie Ihrer Meinung nach …?
How do you plan to …?	Wie planen Sie …?
Could you please explain how …?	Könnten Sie bitte erklären, wie …?
I'd really appreciate it if you could tell me …	Könnten Sie mir bitte sagen …
May I make a suggestion?	Darf ich einen Vorschlag machen?

6	interest-based	['ɪntrəstbeɪst]	interessengeleitet
7 🔊 2.15	to take care of sth	[ˌteɪk 'keər əv]	sich um etw kümmern
	to redo	[riː'duː]	noch einmal tun, neu machen
	bio = biography	['baɪəʊ]	Biografie
8	to let sb off the hook (coll.)	[let ɒf ðə 'hʊk]	jmdm aus der Klemme helfen
	to echo	['ekəʊ]	wiederholen, nachsprechen
9	joint	[dʒɔɪnt]	gemeinsam
	climate change	['klaɪmət tʃeɪndʒ]	Klimawandel
	rise	[raɪz]	Anstieg, Zunahme

Interest-based bargaining

I'd like to hear your perspective on this.	Ich würde gerne Ihren Standpunkt dazu hören.
Perhaps it would be a good idea to …	Es wäre vielleicht eine gute Idee …
So what you're saying is …	Was Sie also sagen wollen, ist …
I'm afraid there's another issue.	Leider gibt es noch ein anderes Problem.
You probably didn't realize, but …	Es ist Ihnen vielleicht nicht bewusst, aber …

8C, Knowing your own culture

◐	to dominate	['dɒmɪneɪt]	dominieren, beherrschen
1	best-selling	[ˌbest'selɪŋ]	häufig verkauft, meistverkauft
	to collide	[kə'laɪd]	zusammenstoßen, aufeinanderprallen
	lengthy	['leŋθi]	übermäßig lang, langatmig
	secrecy	['siːkrəsi]	Geheimhaltung, Verschwiegenheit
	sb lacks sth	[læks]	jmdm fehlt/mangelt es an etw
2	boring	['bɔːrɪŋ]	langweilig
	to stick to sth	[stɪk]	an etw festhalten, bei etw bleiben
	to oversimplify	[ˌəʊvə'sɪmplɪfaɪ]	zu stark vereinfachen
	to lay a foundation	[ˌleɪ ə faʊn'deɪʃn]	eine Grundlage schaffen
	distance of comfort	[ˌdɪstəns əv 'kʌmfət]	Wohlfühlabstand, Sicherheitsabstand
	non-tactile	[ˌnɒn'tæktaɪl]	berührungsarm, berührungslos
3	to empathize with sb	['empəθaɪz wɪð]	sich in jmdn hineinversetzen, jmdm nachfühlen
	truthful	['truːθfl]	ehrlich
	toward	[tə'wɔːd]	in Richtung, gegenüber
	correspondent	[ˌkɒrə'spɒndənt]	Briefschreiber/in
	to place trust in sb	[ˌpleɪs 'trʌst ɪn]	zu jmdm Vertrauen haben, an jmdn glauben
	irony	['aɪrəni]	Ironie
	sarcasm	['sɑːkæzəm]	Sarkasmus
	constructive	[kən'strʌktɪv]	konstruktiv
	head on	[ˌhed 'ɒn]	direkt
	unfinished	[ʌn'fɪnɪʃt]	unvollendet
	hard sell	[ˌhɑːd 'sel]	aggressive Strategie, aggressive Verkaufstaktik
5	observation	[ˌɒbzə'veɪʃn]	Beobachtung
	generalization	[ˌdʒenrəlaɪ'zeɪʃn]	Verallgemeinerung
6	claim	[kleɪm]	Behauptung

8, Extra practice

3	motorway	['məʊtəweɪ]	Autobahn
2.16	to monitor	['mɒnɪtə]	überwachen, kontrollieren
4	to break off	[ˌbreɪk 'ɒf]	abbrechen
	to fall through	[ˌfɔːl 'θruː]	scheitern, nicht zustande kommen
	anxious	['æŋkʃəs]	besorgt, beunruhigt
	mix-up	['mɪksʌp]	Durcheinander, Missverständnis
	to talk business	[ˌtɔːk 'bɪznəs]	Geschäfte machen, über Geschäftliches sprechen
5	negotiating table	[nɪˌgəʊʃieɪtɪŋ 'teɪbl]	Verhandlungstisch
6	to unscramble	[ˌʌn'skræmbl]	entschlüsseln, entwirren
7	to withdraw	[wɪð'drɔː]	zurückziehen, widerrufen
8	valid	['vælɪd]	gültig
CS	to take sth at face value	[teɪk ət ˌfeɪs 'væljuː]	etw für bare Münze nehmen

literally	['lɪtərəli]	wörtlich, buchstäblich
to lose face	[ˌluːz 'feɪs]	das Gesicht verlieren
to go about sth	[tə ˌgəʊ ə'baʊt]	etw anpacken/angehen
early on	[ɜːli 'ɒn]	sehr früh, sehr bald
to test the waters	[test ðə 'wɔːtəz]	die Lage ausloten
savvy (coll.)	['sævi]	schlau, kompetent
frankness	['fræŋknes]	Offenheit, Unbefangenheit

Business file 4 – A negotiation

	to forecast	['fɔːkɑːst]	voraussagen, vorhersagen
1	to call in	[ˌkɔːl 'ɪn]	am Arbeitsplatz anrufen
2.17	shortlist	['ʃɔːtlɪst]	Auswahlliste
	to pass sth	[pɑːs]	etw bestehen
	vendor	['vendə]	Verkäufer/in
	exclusivity	[ˌeksklu:'sɪvəti]	Exklusivität
	to undercut	[ˌʌndə'kʌt]	unterbieten

	consultancy	[kən'sʌltənsi]	Beratungsbüro
	round	[raʊnd]	Runde
2	stability	[stə'bɪləti]	Stabilität
	in turn	[ɪn 'tɜːn]	wiederum
	on purpose	[ɒn 'pɜːpəs]	absichtlich, mit Absicht
	to damage	['dæmɪdʒ]	schädigen, beschädigen
	there's no point in	[ðeəz nəʊ pɔɪnt ɪn]	es hat keinen Zweck, ...
	to squeeze	[skwiːz]	unter Druck setzen
4	non-committal	[ˌnɒnkə'mɪtl]	unverbindlich

9A, A new team

	delegation	[ˌdelɪ'geɪʃn]	Delegieren
2	to disinfect	[ˌdɪsɪn'fekt]	desinfizieren
	ultraviolet	[ˌʌltrə'vaɪələt]	ultraviolett
	to emit	[i'mɪt]	abgeben, freisetzen
	wave	[weɪv]	Welle
	to inactivate	[ɪn'æktɪveɪt]	deaktivieren
	harmful	['hɑːmfl]	schädlich
	micro-organism	[ˌmaɪkrəʊ'ɔːgənɪzəm]	Mikroorganismus
	snapshot	['snæpʃɒt]	Kurzdarstellung
	groundwater	['graʊndwɔːtə]	Grundwasser
	to determine	[dɪ'tɜːmɪn]	bestimmen, prägen
	design criteria	[dɪ'zaɪn kraɪtɪəriə]	Entwicklungskriterien
	large-scale	['lɑːdʒskeɪl]	groß angelegt, in großem Maßstab
	committed	[kə'mɪtɪd]	engagiert

A new team

I just started working for … I will be in charge of / I will be supervising …	Ich habe gerade bei … begonnen. Ich bin verantwortlich für … / werde … beaufsichtigen.
I'm the project leader. I'm responsible for … / It's my job to …	Ich bin die Projektleiterin/der Projektleiter. Ich bin verantwortlich für … / Meine Aufgabe ist …
I'm looking forward to working with you.	Ich freue mich auf die Zusammenarbeit mit Ihnen.

3	tact	[tækt]	Taktgefühl
⏺2.18	now and again	[naʊ ənd əˈgen]	hin und wieder
	Got you.	[ˈgɒt jə]	Verstanden.
	highly	[ˈhaɪli]	sehr, hoch
	unlikely	[ʌnˈlaɪkli]	unwahrscheinlich
	time frame	[ˈtaɪm freɪm]	zeitlicher Rahmen
6	dispersed	[dɪˈspɜːsd]	verteilt, zerstreut
7	duration	[djuˈreɪʃn]	Dauer
⏺2.19	to lay	[leɪ]	verlegen
	it's early days	[ɪts ɜːli ˈdeɪs]	die Sache ist noch im Anfangsstadium; wir sind noch am Anfang
	rock	[rɒk]	Gestein, Fels
	tunnel	[ˈtʌnl]	Tunnel
	to purify	[ˈpjʊərɪfaɪ]	reinigen
	purification	[ˌpjʊərɪfɪˈkeɪʃn]	Reinigung
	commissioning	[kəˈmɪʃənɪŋ]	Inbetriebnahme, Abnahmetest
	municipal	[mjuːˈnɪsɪpl]	Gemeinde-, Stadt-, städtisch
	to rebuild	[ˌriːˈbɪld]	wieder aufbauen
8	throughout	[θruːˈaʊt]	die ganze Zeit hindurch
	in progress	[ɪn ˈprəʊgres]	im Gange
9	equipment	[ɪˈkwɪpmənt]	Anlage
	to oversee	[ˌəʊvəˈsiː]	überwachen, beaufsichtigen
	Gantt chart	[ˈgænt tʃɑːt]	Gantt-Diagramm, Zeitplan

9B, A progress report

▶	to run over schedule	[ˌrʌn əʊvə ˈʃedjuːl]	den Zeitplan nicht einhalten, im Verzug sein
1	greenfield site	[ˈgriːnfiːld saɪt]	nicht erschlossenes Baugrundstück, grüne Wiese
	forest	[ˈfɒrɪst]	Wald
	undeveloped	[ˌʌndɪˈveləpt]	nicht erschlossen
	to develop	[dɪˈveləp]	erschließen
	urban	[ˈɜːbən]	Stadt-, städtisch
	wildlife	[ˈwaɪldlaɪf]	Tierwelt
	dweller	[ˈdwelə]	Bewohner/in
	bar	[bɑː]	Stab, Stange, Balken
2	robotic	[rəʊˈbɒtɪk]	Roboter-

Work is currently in progress on …	Im Moment wird an … gearbeitet.
Work is progressing well / is nearing completion.	Die Arbeiten gehen gut voran / stehen kurz vor dem Abschluss.
Up to now / So far, … has been completed.	Bis jetzt / Bisher wurde … fertiggestellt.
Work has already commenced / begun on …	Die Arbeit mit/an … hat schon begonnen.
No progress has yet been made on …	Bei … wurde bislang noch kein Fortschritt erzielt.
It is anticipated that … will be completed in the next two months.	… wird voraussichtlich in den nächsten zwei Monaten fertiggestellt.
The project is on / behind schedule.	Die Arbeiten am Projekt liegen im / hinter dem Zeitplan.
The project is within / over the budget.	Die Kosten für das Projekt liegen im / über dem Budget.

6	to come up against sth	[ˌkʌm ˈʌp əgenst]	auf etw stoßen
	to near	[nɪə]	sich nähern
	filter	[ˈfɪltə]	Filter
	nozzle	[ˈnɒzl]	Düse
	to commence	[kəˈmens]	beginnen
	setback	[ˈsetbæk]	Rückschlag
	in the interim	[ɪn ðiː ˈɪntərɪm]	in der Zwischenzeit
	to assure	[əˈʃʊə]	versichern, gewährleisten
	to expedite	[ˈekspədaɪt]	beschleunigen
	lifting equipment	[ˈlɪftɪŋ ɪkwɪpmənt]	Hebevorrichtung, Hubgerät
7	to envisage sth	[ɪnˈvɪzɪdʒ]	etw voraussehen, etw planen
8	nature	[ˈneɪtʃə]	Art, Wesen
9	lift	[lɪft]	Mitfahrgelegenheit
10	to juggle	[ˈdʒʌgl]	jonglieren
	expectation	[ˌekspekˈteɪʃn]	Erwartung
	rubber	[ˈrʌbə]	Gummi

Dealing with favours

Would you mind doing me a favour?	Könnten Sie mir einen Gefallen tun?
– I'd be glad to. / I'm very sorry, but I'm afraid I won't be able to.	– Sehr gerne. / Es tut mir wirklich leid, aber ich kann leider nicht.
Would you be so kind to help me?	Wären Sie so freundlich, mir zu helfen?
– Yes, no problem. / I'd like to say yes, but …	– Ja, kein Problem. / Ich würde gerne, aber …
It would be great if you could …	Es wäre toll, wenn Sie … könnten.

9C, Delegating

1 picky	['pɪki]	wählerisch, pingelig
to be better off	[bi betər 'ɒf]	besser dran sein
to check in	[ˌtʃek 'ɪn]	überprüfen
up front	[ʌp 'frɒnt]	im Voraus
to pop in (coll.)	[ˌpɒp 'ɪn]	vorbeischauen
day job	['deɪ dʒɒb]	Hauptberuf, Job
newborn	['njuːbɔːn]	Neugeborenes
to micromanage	['maɪkrəʊmænɪdʒ]	sich in Details einmischen
freedom	['friːdəm]	Freiheit
to see fit	[siː 'fɪt]	es für richtig halten, es für angebracht halten
patch (coll.)	[pætʃ]	hier: Phase

Delegating

Some people are picky about …	Einige Leute sind sehr pingelig bei …
You're probably better off handling … yourself.	Sie tun wahrscheinlich besser daran, … selbst zu erledigen.
Don't assign too much.	Geben Sie nicht zu viele Anweisungen.
Get the job done as you see fit.	Erledigen Sie die Aufgabe nach eigenem Ermessen.

2 unannounced	[ˌʌnə'naʊnst]	unangekündigt
3 usefulness	['juːsfəlnəs]	Nützlichkeit, Eignung
beneficial	[ˌbenɪ'fɪʃl]	vorteilhaft, nützlich

9, Grammar summary

overdue	[ˌəʊvə'djuː]	überfällig

9, Extra practice

4 first-time	[ˌfɜːst 'taɪm]	erstmalig, neu-
cs turn-taking	['tɜːn teɪkɪŋ]	Sprecherwechsel
to clash	[klæʃ]	zusammenstoßen, aufeinanderprallen
to keep doing sth	[kiːp 'duːɪŋ]	etw immer weiter tun
on hand	[ɒn 'hænd]	bereit, zur Verfügung
to cope	[kəʊp]	zurechtkommen
to beg sb's pardon	[beg 'pɑːdn]	jmdn um Verzeihung bitten
to converse	[kən'vɜːs]	sich unterhalten
index finger	['ɪndeks fɪŋgə]	Zeigefinger
by accident	[baɪ 'æksɪdent]	aus Versehen
to get a word in edgewise	[get ə ˌwɜːd ɪn 'edʒwaɪz]	auch mal zu Wort kommen

10A, The perfect product

1	sales performance	['seɪlz pəfɔːməns]	Verkaufsergebnis, Absatz
	poll	[pəʊl]	Umfrage
	intensively	[ɪn'tensɪvli]	intensiv, eingehend
	following	['fɒləʊɪŋ]	nach
2	upscale	[ˌʌp'skeɪl]	exklusiv, gehoben
	fragrance	['freɪɡrəns]	Duft, Parfum
	casual	['kæʒuəl]	lässig, unaufdringlich
	scent	[sent]	Duft, Parfum
	collection	[kə'lekʃn]	Sammlung, Kollektion
	apparel	[ə'pærəl]	Kleidung, Bekleidung
	sponsorship	['spɒnsəʃɪp]	finanzielle Förderung
	profile	['prəʊfaɪl]	Image
	value management	['vælju: mænɪdʒmənt]	Wertmanagement

🔊 2.20

3	suspense	[sə'spens]	Spannung
	to keep sb in suspense	[kiːp ɪn sə'spens]	jmdn auf die Folter spannen
	auditorium	[ˌɔːdɪ'tɔːriəm]	Vortragssaal
	affiliate	[ə'fɪlieɪt]	Filiale
	knowledgeable	['nɒlɪdʒəbl]	kompetent, versiert
	passionate	['pæʃənət]	leidenschaftlich

Developping a new product

... is closely monitored to improve ...	... wird genau überprüft, um ... zu verbessern.
... is analysed by ...	... wird analysiert, indem ...
Ideas for new ... are generated.	Es werden Ideen für neue ... entwickelt.
... is tested on the market / launched.	... wird auf dem Markt getestet / auf den Markt gebracht.

4	consistent	[kən'sɪstənt]	beständig
	edutainment	[edʒu'teɪnmənt]	spielerisches Lernen, Kombination aus Unterhaltung und Wissenserwerb
	one of a kind	[wʌn əv ə 'kaɪnd]	einzigartig, einmalig

5 🔊 2.21

	pilot project	['paɪlət prɒdʒəkt]	Pilotprojekt, Modellversuch
6	business services IT	[bɪznəs 'sɜːvɪsəs aɪ tiː]	IT-Dienstleister
	to modify	['mɒdɪfaɪ]	verändern
8	chemist	['kemɪst]	Chemiker/in
	Nobel Prize	[nəʊˌbel 'praɪz]	Nobelpreis

10B, Brainstorming solutions

1	terms of reference	[ˌtɜːmz əv 'refrəns]	*hier:* Referenz, Bezug, Hintergrundinformation
	to appear	[ə'pɪə]	scheinen, erscheinen
	brand recognition	['brænd rekəgnɪʃn]	Wiedererkennung einer Marke, Markenbewusstsein
	into	['ɪntə]	zu
	inferior	[ɪn'fɪəriə]	minderwertig
	to offend	[ə'fend]	beleidigen
	questioner	['kwestʃənə]	Fragesteller/in
	advisable	[əd'vaɪzəbl]	ratsam
	one-to-one	[ˌwʌn tə 'wʌn]	von Angesicht zu Angesicht, persönlich
2	dispenser	[dɪ'spensə]	Sprühflasche
	rebranding	[ˌriː'brændɪŋ]	ein neues Markenimage geben, einen neuen Markennamen geben
	pocket-sized	['pɒkɪt saɪzd]	im Taschenformat
	mist	[mɪst]	Nebel, Dunst
	unforeseen	[ˌʌnfɔː'siːn]	unvorhergesehen, unerwartet
3	non-aerosol	[ˌnɒn 'eərəsɒl]	aerosolfrei
2.22	biochemist	[ˌbaɪəʊ'kemɪst]	Biochemiker/in
	protection	[prə'tekʃn]	Schutz
	consumer protection agency	[kənsjuːmə 'prətekʃn eɪdʒənsi]	Verbraucherschutzorganisation
	promotion	[prə'məʊʃn]	*hier:* Werbung, Werbeaktion
	freebie	['friːbi]	Werbegeschenk
	last-minute	[ˌlɑːst 'mɪnɪt]	in letzter Minute, kurzfristig
	item	['aɪtəm]	Artikel, Gegenstand
	to keep an eye on sb	[kiːp ən 'aɪ ɒn]	ein Auge auf jmdn haben, auf jmdn aufpassen
	easier said than done	[iːziə ˌsed ðən 'dʌn]	leichter gesagt als getan
	sub-supplier	[ˌsʌbsə'plaɪə]	Zulieferer, Sublieferant
	flop	[flɒp]	Reinfall
4	board	[bɔːd]	Vorstand
2.23	toy	[tɔɪ]	Spielzeug
	to kill two birds with one stone	[kɪl tuː ˌbɜːdz wɪð wʌn 'stəʊn]	zwei Fliegen mit einer Klappe schlagen
	to nod	[nɒd]	nicken
5	quote *(coll.)*	[kwəʊt]	Zitat
	to uphold	[ʌp'həʊld]	unterstützen, bestätigen
	by chance	[baɪ 'tʃɑːns]	zufällig
6	in summary	[ɪn 'sʌməri]	zusammenfassend

Writing a report

This report was requested by …	Dieser Bericht wurde von … angefragt.
The aim of this report is to …	Ziel dieses Berichts ist …
We discovered that …	Wir haben herausgefunden, dass …
This might be due to the fact that …	Dies könnte an … liegen.
Nevertheless … / In addition … / Otherwise …	Dennoch … / Des Weiteren … / Sonst …
It is essential that we …	Es kommt darauf an, dass wir …
We therefore recommend …	Deshalb empfehlen wir …
It is advisable to …	Es empfiehlt sich …

7			
	provocative	[prə'vɒkətɪv]	provozierend
	generic	[dʒə'nerɪk]	*hier:* allgemein
	polite noise	[pə͵laɪt 'nɔɪz]	höfliche Bemerkung
	absenteeism	[͵æbsen'tiːɪzəm]	häufiges unentschuldigtes Fehlen, Schwänzen
	to hold back	[͵həʊld 'bæk]	zurückhalten
	to elaborate on sth	[ɪ'læbərət ɒn]	etw näher ausführen
	to measure	['meʒə]	messen

Brainstorming ideas

What do you think we should do about …?	Was sollten wir Ihrer Meinung nach bezüglich … machen?
I'd appreciate everyone's opinion here on …	Ich würde gern die Meinung aller zu … hören.
Please feel free to give your honest opinions and don't hold back.	Bitte sagen Sie Ihre ehrliche Meinung und halten Sie sich nicht zurück.
Could you elaborate a bit on that perspective, please?	Könnten Sie Ihren Standpunkt bitte etwas genauer erläutern?

8			
	given	['gɪvn]	bestimmt, vorgegeben
	to tell time	[͵tel 'taɪm]	die Uhr lesen
	to transfer	[træns'fɜː]	übertragen
	chair	[tʃeə]	Vorsitzende/r

10C, Professional communities

○	community	[kə'mjuːnəti]	Gemeinschaft
	advance	[əd'vɑːns]	Fortschritt
	peer	[pɪə]	Fachkollege, Fachkollegin
1	numerous	['njuːmərəs]	zahlreich
	to further	['fɜːðə]	fördern
	methodology	[͵meθə'dɒlədʒi]	Methodologie, Methodik
	certification	[͵sɜːtɪfɪ'keɪʃn]	Zulassung, Zertifizierung
	need	[niːd]	Bedarf

engineering	[ˌendʒɪˈnɪərɪŋ]	Ingenieurwesen, Maschinenbau
electrical engineering	[ɪˌlektrɪkl endʒɪˈnɪərɪŋ]	Elektrotechnik
predefined	[ˌpriːdɪˈfaɪnd]	im Voraus bestimmt, im Voraus festgelegt
best practice	[ˌbest ˈpræktɪs]	optimales Vorgehen, vorbildliches Verfahren
across	[əˈkrɒs]	in
forward	[ˈfɔːwəd]	Voraus-
to set aside	[ˌset əˈsaɪd]	zur Seite legen, einplanen
2 to raise	[reɪz]	zur Sprache bringen, erwähnen
growth rate	[ˈɡrəʊθ reɪt]	Wachstumsrate
to draw a conclusion	[ˌdrɔː ə kənˈkluːʒn]	einen Schluss ziehen
3 interface	[ˈɪntəfeɪs]	Schnittstelle
to keep sb posted	[kiːp ˈpəʊstɪd]	jmdn auf dem Laufenden halten
to outweigh	[ˌaʊtˈweɪ]	überwiegen

Professional communities ...

... connect with peers at face-to-face events.	... nehmen bei Veranstaltungen Kontakt mit Fachkollegen auf.
... are formally organized with restricted membership.	... sind organisiert und haben eine begrenzte Zahl an Mitgliedern.
... discuss specific challenges.	... diskutieren über spezifische Herausforderungen.
... come up with solutions for best practice.	... schlagen Lösungen für ein optimales Vorgehen vor.

10, Grammar summary

| for sure *(coll.)* | [fə ˈʃʊə] | ganz sicher, ganz bestimmt |

10, Extra practice

2.24

release	[rɪˈliːs]	Herausbringen, Neuerscheinung
4 effort	[ˈefət]	Anstrengung, Mühe
record	[ˈrekɔːd]	Rekord
6 hurdle	[ˈhɜːdl]	Hürde
CS viewpoint	[ˈvjuːpɔɪnt]	Standpunkt, Blickwinkel
unsure	[ˌʌnˈʃʊə]	unsicher
to strike sb as	[straɪk əz]	jmdm als ... vorkommen
to deliver	[dɪˈlɪvə]	überbringen
insensitive	[ɪnˈsensətɪv]	gefühllos, unsensibel
unwilling	[ʌnˈwɪlɪŋ]	nicht bereit, widerwillig
modification	[ˌmɒdɪfɪˈkeɪʃn]	Änderung, Modifikation
to put sb at ease	[pʊt ət ˈiːz]	jmdm seine Befangenheit nehmen

I think perhaps we could do things this way.	Wir könnten es vielleicht so machen.
This is the way we should do things.	So sollten wir es machen.
This is quite a good approach.	Das ist ein ziemlich guter Ansatz.
Don't you think we should also consider …?	Sollten wir nicht auch … in Betracht ziehen?

Business file 5 – At a trade fair

2	to hand out	[ˌhænd 'aut]	aushändigen, verteilen
	line	[laɪn]	*hier:* Branche
	audit	['ɔːdɪt]	Untersuchung, Prüfung
	usage	['juːsɪdʒ]	Verbrauch
	reduction	[rɪ'dʌkʃn]	Reduktion, Verminderung
	geothermal	[ˌdʒiːəʊ'θɜːml]	geothermal, Erdwärme-
3	spy	[spaɪ]	Spion
	sponsor	['spɒnsə]	Sponsor/in
	coach	[kəʊtʃ]	Trainer/in
	jersey	['dʒɜːzi]	Trikot
	to renovate	['renəveɪt]	renovieren
	to play sports	[ˌpleɪ 'spɔːts]	Sport treiben
	publicity	[pʌb'lɪsəti]	Werbung, Publicity
5	to make reference to	[ˌmeɪk 'refrəns tə]	Bezug nehmen auf
	rep = representative	[rep]	Vertreter/in

Business correspondence

1	reminder	[rɪ'maɪndə]	Erinnerung, Mahnung
	seldom	['seldəm]	selten
	greeting	['griːtɪŋ]	Gruß, Begrüßung
	salutation	[ˌsælju'teɪʃn]	Begrüßung, Anrede
	letterhead	['letəhed]	Briefkopf
	sender	['sendə]	Absender/in
	recipient	[rɪ'sɪpiənt]	Empfänger/in
	inside address	[ɪnˌsaɪd ə'dres]	hausinterne Adresse
	body of letter	[ˌbɒdi əv 'letə]	Hauptteil eines Briefes
	complimentary close	[kɒmplɪˌmentri 'kləʊz]	Grußformel, Schlussformel
	enclosure	[ɪn'kləʊʒə]	Anlage
	starter application form	['staːtər æplɪkeɪʃn fɔːm]	Erstantrag
	Yours truly	[ˌjɔːz 'truːli]	Mit freundlichen Grüßen
	to whom it may concern	[tə ˌhuːm ɪt meɪ kən's3ːn]	an die zuständige Abteilung
	common	['kɒmən]	weit verbreitet, häufig
	to watch sth	[wɒtʃ]	auf etw achten
	colon	['kəʊlən]	Doppelpunkt
	capital letter	[ˌkæpɪtəl 'letə]	Großbuchstabe
	press release	['pres rɪliːs]	Pressemitteilung, Presseerklärung

	advice	[əd'vaıs]	*hier:* Benachrichtigung, Hinweis
	to justify	['dʒʌstıfaı]	rechtfertigen, begründen
2	carbon copy = cc	[ˌkɑːbən 'kɒpı]	Durchschlag, Kopie
	to cover for sb	['kʌvə fə]	für jmdn einspringen
	return	[rı'tɜːn]	Rückkehr
	out of office reply	[aʊt əv ˌɒfıs rı'plaı]	Abwesenheitsnachricht/-notiz
	distinction	[dı'stıŋkʃn]	Unterschied, Unterscheidung
	follow-on	[ˌfɒləʊ 'ɒn]	Folge-
	equal	['iːkwəl]	gleichberechtigt
	exchange	[ıks'tʃeındʒ]	Austausch
	cheers *(coll.)*	[tʃıəz]	tschüs
	humble	['hʌmbl]	bescheiden
3	forensic	[fə'rensık]	forensisch, gerichts-
	investigation	[ınˌvestı'geıʃn]	Ermittlung, Recherche
	Re = regarding	[riː]	Betreff, betreffend
	replacement	[rı'pleısmənt]	Ersatz, Auswechseln
	budgetary restriction	['bʌdʒıtəri rıstrıkʃn]	Haushaltseinsparungen, Sparmaßnahmen
	to progress	[prə'gres]	vorankommen, Fortschritte machen
	hopefully	['həʊpfəli]	hoffentlich
	in the course of	[ın ðə 'kɔːs əv]	im Laufe von
	as opposed to	[əz ə'pəʊzd tə]	im Gegensatz zu
	to multiply	['mʌltiplaı]	vervielfachen
	to dictate	[dık'teıt]	diktieren, bestimmen
	to delete	[dı'liːt]	löschen
	to apply	[ə'plaı]	zutreffen, gelten
4	to spend	[spend]	*hier:* ausgeben
	unchanged	[ʌn'tʃeındʒd]	unverändert
	postage	['pəʊstıdʒ]	Porto
	on receipt	[ɒn rı'siːt]	bei Erhalt
5	stainless	['steınləs]	rostfrei
	threaded rod	[ˌθredəd 'rɒd]	Gewindestange
	dome nut	['dəʊm nʌt]	Hutmutter
	half nut	['hɑːf nʌt]	halbe Mutter
	hose clip	['həʊz klıp]	Schlauchschelle
	band	[bænd]	Band, Bund
	diameter	[daı'æmıtə]	Durchmesser
	flat washer	['flæt wɒʃə]	Unterlegscheibe
	flour	['flaʊə]	Mehl
6	in the first instance	[ın ðə 'fɜːst ınstəns]	zunächst einmal
	to settle	['setl]	ausgleichen, bezahlen
	outstanding	[aʊt'stændıŋ]	ausstehend
	settlement	['setlmənt]	Ausgleich, Bezahlung
	to clear	[klıə]	*hier:* begleichen
	to resolve	[rı'sɒlv]	lösen, klären
	to disregard	[ˌdısrı'gɑːd]	ignorieren, nicht beachten
	to a certain extent	[tu ə sɜːtən ık'stent]	bis zu einem gewissen Grad, gewissermaßen

7	horizontal	[ˌhɒrɪ'zɒntl]	horizontal
	vertical	['vɜːtɪkl]	vertikal
	banner	['bænə]	Transparent, Spruchband, (Messe)Aufsteller
	on	[ɒn]	bei
	misprint	['mɪsprɪnt]	Fehldruck
	auto-correction	[ˌɔːtəʊkə'rekʃn]	automatische Fehlerkorrektur
	custom	['kʌstəm]	Kundschaft
	to correspond	[ˌkɒrə'spɒnd]	entsprechen, übereinstimmen
	standing	['stændɪŋ]	Rang, Ansehen
	shortly	['ʃɔːtli]	in Kürze, bald
	fire extinguisher	['faɪər ɪkstɪŋgwɪʃə]	Feuerlöscher
	believable	[bɪ'liːvəbl]	glaubhaft
	impersonal	[ɪm'pɜːsənl]	unpersönlich
	to attack	[ə'tæk]	angreifen, attackieren
8	condolence	[kən'dəʊləns]	Beileid, Kondolenz
	regret	[rɪ'gret]	Bedauern
	to miss	[mɪs]	vermissen
	to extend sth to sb	[ɪk'stend tə]	jmdm etw ausrichten
	sad	[sæd]	traurig
	to reflect	[rɪ'flekt]	spiegeln, reflektieren
	emotion	[ɪ'məʊʃn]	Gefühl
	bookkeeper	['bʊkkiːpə]	Buchhalter/in
	to assume	[ə'sjuːm]	übernehmen
	grandchildren	['græntʃɪldrən]	Enkelkinder

Alphabetical register

In der folgenden Liste finden Sie die Einträge der chronologischen Liste in alphabetischer Reihenfolge. Einträge, die aus mehreren Wörtern bestehen, sind mehrfach aufgelistet, und zwar unter den jeweiligen Anfangsbuchstaben ihrer einzelnen Bestandteile (ausgenommen Präpositionen oder ähnliche Funktionswörter). Beispiel: Der Eintrag *crushed stone* ist sowohl unter 'c' als auch unter 's' aufgelistet; *to buy up* hingegen steht nur unter 'b'.

A

to abandon **16** aufgeben

absenteeism **131** häufiges unentschuldigtes Fehlen, Schwänzen

absolutely **51** absolut, sicher

to absorb **75** aufnehmen

abstention **51** Stimmenthaltung, Enthaltung

acceptance **28** Akzeptanz, Zustimmung

limited access **58** beschränkter Zugang

to gain access **88** Zugang erhalten

accessible **80** zugänglich

accident **26** Unfall

by accident **125** aus Versehen

accidentally **53** versehentlich

to accomplish **62** erreichen

accuracy **61** Genauigkeit

achievable **55** erreichbar, realisierbar

phosphoric acid **88** Phosphorsäure

to acknowledge **69** anerkennen, bestätigen

acknowledgement **69** Anerkennung

a couple of **22** ein paar

acquisition **13** Akquisition

across **132** in

to get a message across **62** eine Aussage vermitteln

action plan **38** Maßnahmenplan

action items **86** offene Punkte, umzusetzende Maßnahmen

out of action **26** außer Gefecht

course of action **86** Vorgehen, Handlungsschritt

adaptor plug **62** Adapterstecker

in addition **88** zusätzlich

to address sth to sb **78** etw an jmdn richten

inside address **156** hausinterne Adresse

adequate **55** ausreichend, angemessen

to adjourn **59** vertagen, unterbrechen

to adjust **6** einstellen

to admire **17** bewundern, schätzen

to admit **26** zugeben, eingestehen

to adopt **66** annehmen, übernehmen

advance **132** Fortschritt

adventure **42** Abenteuer

advice **157** *hier:* Benachrichtigung, Hinweis

advisable **129** ratsam

adviser **47** Berater/in

non-aerosol **130** aerosolfrei

affiliate **127** Filiale

afloat **16** über Wasser

EMEA = Europe, Middle East, Africa **80** Wirtschaftsraum Europa, Naher Osten, Afrika

after all **97** letzten Endes, schließlich

now and again **115** hin und wieder

consumer protection agency **130** Verbraucherschutzorganisation

to take ages **60** eine Ewigkeit dauern

aggregate **75** Betonzuschlag

go-ahead **100** grünes Licht

ahead of **101** vor, voraus

to think ahead **81** vorausdenken, vorausplanen

to **aim at sth** **74** etw beabsichtigen,
etw anstreben
alert **72** aufmerksam, munter
alive **68** am Leben, lebendig
at all **49** überhaupt
after all **97** letzten Endes, schließlich
to **allocate** **55** bestimmen, zuweisen
let alone **13** geschweige denn
to **go along with sb** **6** jmdn begleiten
alternative **24** Alternative
amazed **100** erstaunt, verwundert
ambition **68** Ambition, Ehrgeiz
ambitious **46** ehrgeizig, ambitioniert
among **52** zwischen, unter, inmitten
amount **13** Menge
SWOT analysis (SWOT = Strengths,
Weaknesses, Opportunities and
Threats) 34 Stärken-Schwächen-
Analyse
anecdote **67** Anekdote, persönlicher Bericht
angle **61** Blickwinkel, Perspektive
ankle **26** Fußknöchel
annoying **100** lästig, ärgerlich
Q&A = question and answer **83** Frage
und Antwort
anxious **109** besorgt, beunruhigt
apart from **13** außer
Please accept my apologies for ... 22
Bitte entschuldigen Sie, dass ...
to **send one's apologies** **37** sich
entschuldigen lassen
apparel **126** Kleidung, Bekleidung
to **appear** **129** scheinen, erscheinen
appliance **62** Gerät
applicable **133** anwendbar, zutreffend
starter application form **156** Erstantrag
to **apply** **162** zutreffen, gelten
to **apply for** **72** beantragen
to **appoint** **37** ernennen
approach **17** Annäherung
to **approach sb** **88** an jmdn herantreten
area sales manager **13** Gebietsverkaufs-
leiter/in

to **crowd around** **50** sich drängen
works of art **26** Kunstwerke
to **ask sb out for dinner** **24** jmdn zum
Essen einladen
to **fall asleep** **54** einschlafen
as opposed to **162** im Gegensatz zu
to **kick one's ass** *(coll.)* **69** jmdm in den
Hintern treten
assembly **87** Montage
cable assembly **16** Leitung, Kabel-
montage
to **assess** **50** einschätzen, beurteilen
to **assign sb** **48** jmdn beauftragen, jmdn
zuteilen
associate **34** Kollege, Kollegin,
Mitarbeiter/in
to **assume** **170** übernehmen
assumption **55** Annahme, Vermutung
to **assure** **118** versichern, gewährleisten
at all **49** überhaupt
at once **49** sofort
to **attack** **169** angreifen, attackieren
to **launch an attack at sb** **55** einen
Angriff auf jmdn starten
attempt **16** Versuch
attendance **51** Anwesenheit, Teilnehmer-
zahl
to **pay attention** **50** aufpassen,
aufmerksam sein
to **bring sth to sb's attention** **55** jmdn
auf etw aufmerksam machen
to **grab sb's attention** **62** jmds
Aufmerksamkeit auf sich ziehen
to **call attention** **92** Aufmerksamkeit
erregen
attitude **29** Einstellung, Haltung
to **attribute** **29** zuschreiben
auction **86** Auktion
reverse auction **86** Ausschreibung
audit **138** Untersuchung, Prüfung
auditor **22** Rechnungsprüfer/in, Prüfer/in
auditorium **127** Vortragssaal
authentic **26** echt, originalgetreu

auto-correction **168** automatische Fehlerkorrektur

automation **6** Automatisierung

avid **68** begeistert, leidenschaftlich

to award **42** verleihen

to award **53** *hier:* zuerkennen

awful **35** schrecklich

B

to back up sth **81** eine Sicherheitskopie von etw anlegen; *hier:* etw erläutern, etw belegen

back seat **81** Rücksitz, Rückbank

backwards **38** rückwärts, von hinten nach vorn

to be of bad quality **39** von schlechter Qualität sein

to put the ball in sb's court **47** jmdm den Ball zuwerfen/zuspielen

to throw a curve ball **47** (mit einer Frage) überrumpeln

to ban **54** verbieten, sperren

band **164** Band, Bund

banner **168** Transparent, Spruchband, (Messe)Aufsteller

bar chart **74** Balkendiagramm

bar **117** Balken, Stab, Stange

interest-based **105** interessengeleitet

basic **87** einfach, grundlegend

basic chemical **88** Grundchemikalie, chemischer Grundstoff

battle **91** Kampf

to be in charge of **13** leiten

to be to do sth **88** etw tun sollen

bear in mind **92** denken Sie daran; vergessen Sie nicht

bear with so **13** mit jmdm Geduld haben, mit jmdm nachsichtig sein

to become comfortable **21** sich wohl fühlen

to beg sb's pardon **125** jmdn um Verzeihung bitten

to behave **29** sich benehmen, sich verhalten

behaviour **53** Benehmen, Verhalten

to be in a hurry **50** in Eile sein, es eilig haben

belief **29** Überzeugung, Glaube

believable **169** glaubhaft

bell **37** Glocke

to ring a bell *(coll.)* **37** bekannt vorkommen

benchmark **95** Maßstab

beneficial **121** vorteilhaft, nützlich

beside **13** neben

best-selling **106** häufig verkauft, meistverkauft

best practice **132** optimales Vorgehen, vorbildliches Verfahren

to be better off **120** besser dran sein

to get better at **6** besser werden in

to change for the better **78** sich zum Besseren verändern

bewildered **100** verwirrt, verwundert

bewildering **100** verwirrend

to be beyond the scope of sth **37** außerhalb des Rahmens von etw liegen, den Rahmen von etw sprengen

to bid **86** bieten, ein Angebot machen

bilingual **40** zweisprachig

billionaire **68** Milliardär/in

bio = biography **105** Biografie

biochemist **130** Biochemiker/in

biocidal **88** biozid

biocide **88** Biozid, Pestizid

to kill two birds with one stone **130** zwei Fliegen mit einer Klappe schlagen

quite a bit **35** ziemlich viel

blackjack **42** *Kartenspiel:* Siebzehnundvier

to blacklist **87** auf die schwarze Liste setzen

to go blank **13** einen Blackout haben

board **130** Vorstand

regulatory board **86** Aufsichtsrat, Aufsichtsgremium

printed circuit board **86** Leiterplatte, Platine

body of letter **156** Hauptteil eines Briefes

boiler **14** Boiler, Heizkessel

in bold **92** fett gedruckt

to bond **55** *hier:* verbinden, zusammen-
schweißen

bookkeeper **170** Buchhalter/in

border **78** Grenze

to bore **70** langweilen

boring **106** langweilig

to bother **64** sich kümmern

bottleneck **78** Engpass; Flaschenhals

bottleneck point **78** Engpass, Engstelle

bottom line **89** Fazit, das Entscheidende

time-bound **55** fristgebunden

brand recognition **129** Wiedererkennung
einer Marke, Markenbewusstsein

to break off **109** abbrechen

short break **26** Kurzurlaub

comfort break **55** kurze Pause

breakdown **28** Störung, Zusammenbruch

breath **85** Atem, Atemzug

to breed **79** hervorrufen, brüten

to brief **9** informieren, instruieren

brief **38** Briefing, Einweisung

to bring sth to sb's attention **55** jmdn
auf etw aufmerksam machen

to bring up **92** ansprechen, erwähnen

to bring in **96** zum Einsatz bringen, ein-
bringen

brisk **99** brüsk, lebhaft

Brit *(coll.)* **101** Brite, Britin

broad **104** breit, ausgedehnt

brush-off **59** Absage

brutal **59** brutal, knallhart

budgetary restriction **161** Haushalts-
einsparungen, Sparmaßnahmen

self-serve buffet **104** Selbstbedienungsbuffet

build up **69** Aufbau

builder **26** Bauarbeiter/in

building **78** Bau

team-building **42** Teamentwicklung

in-built **81** eingebaut

bullet point **63** Aufzählungszeichen

to bump into sb **11** jmdn zufällig treffen

business entertaining **6** Geschäfts-
veranstaltungen

business unit manager **15** Leiter/in des
Geschäftsbereichs

business development **34** Akquisition,
Geschäftsentwicklung

B2B = Business-to-business **36**
Geschäftsbeziehungen zwischen
Unternehmen

business traveler **80** Geschäftsreisende/r

business etiquette **102** Geschäftsetikette

business services IT **128** IT-Dienstleister

to talk business **109** Geschäfte machen,
über Geschäftliches sprechen

butterfly **25** Schmetterling

social butterfly **25** Partygänger/in

to buy up **90** aufkaufen

by accident **125** aus Versehen

C

cabinet **30** Schrank

storage cabinet **30** Lagerschrank, Datenschutzschrank

cable assembly **16** Leitung, Kabelmon-
tage

call **36** Aufruf

call for tenders **36** Ausschreibung

call **37** *hier:* Gespräch

to call for **36** erfordern, verlangen

to call attention **92** Aufmerksamkeit erregen

to call in **112** am Arbeitsplatz anrufen

canvas **42** Leinwand

capability **16** Fähigkeit

capacity **38** Kapazität, Leistungsvermögen

to reach capacity **38** mit voller Leistung
arbeiten

capital letter **157** Großbuchstabe

carbon footprint **66** CO_2-Bilanz

carbon copy = cc **158** Durchschlag, Kopie

to take care of sth **105** sich um etw
kümmern

to carry a risk **84** ein Risiko bergen,
risikobehaftet sein

case study **28** Fallstudie

worst case scenario **77** der schlimmste Fall, größter anzunehmender Unfall – GAU

cash register **37** Kasse

casual **126** lässig, unaufdringlich

cause **49** Grund, Ursache

caution **50** Vorsicht, Warnung

cautious **76** vorsichtig

celebration **42** Feier

celebrity **43** berühmte Persönlichkeit

cement **74** Zement

per cent **38** Prozent

central **11** zentral

to centralize **87** zentralisieren

to a certain extent **167** bis zu einem gewissen Grad, gewissermaßen

certification **132** Zulassung, Zertifizierung

to certify **87** zertifizieren, bescheinigen

chain of command **16** Befehlskette, Dienstweg

chair **131** Vorsitzende/r

chamber of commerce **78** Handelskammer

by chance **130** zufällig

to change for the better **78** sich zum Besseren verändern

to change for the worse **78** sich zum Schlechteren verändern

climate change **105** Klimawandel

channel **16** Kanal, Sender

channel of communication **16** Kommunikationsweg

chaotic **13** chaotisch

to be in charge of **13** leiten

charitable **68** gemeinnützig, wohltätig

charity **68** Wohltätigkeits-

pie chart **7** Tortendiagramm

bar chart **74** Balkendiagramm

flow chart **74** Flussdiagramm

Gantt chart **116** Gantt-Diagramm, Zeitplan

check **48** Überprüfung, Kontrolle

preventative check **48** Wartung

to check in **29** *hier:* ankommen

to check in **120** überprüfen

to check up on sth **92** etw überprüfen

checklist **37** Checkliste, Prüfliste

security checkpoint **80** Sicherheitskontrolle

cheers *(coll.)* **159** tschüs

basic chemical **88** Grundchemikalie, chemischer Grundstoff

chemist **128** Chemiker/in

chemistry **102** Chemie

Chief Information Officer (= CIO) **6** Leiter/in der Abteilung Informationstechnologie

chief **13** Häuptling

chief **102** Haupt-

There are too many chiefs and not enough Indians. *(coll.)* **13** Es gibt zu viele Leute, die Befehle erteilen, und nicht genug Leute, die die Arbeit machen.

circuit **86** Stromkreis

printed circuit board **86** Leiterplatte, Platine

circumstances **64** Umstände, Verhältnisse

claim **107** Behauptung

clarification **38** Klärung, Klarstellung

clarity **93** Klarheit, Direktheit

clash **29** Zusammenstoß

to clash **125** zusammenstoßen, aufeinanderprallen

to clear **167** begleichen

to clear up **53** aufklären

Did I make myself clear? **38** Haben Sie mich verstanden?, Habe ich mich verständlich ausgedrückt?

climate change **105** Klimawandel

to climb up **43** hochklettern

hose clip **164** Schlauchschelle

closed question **103** Entscheidungsfrage

coach **138** Trainer/in

coating **88** Beschichtung

to enhance the code **53** den Code verbessern

collaboration **89** Zusammenarbeit

collaboratively **99** gemeinsam

collection **126** Sammlung, Kollektion

to collide **106** zusammenstoßen, aufeinanderprallen

colon **157** Doppelpunkt

to combine **15** kombinieren, verbinden

to come away with **42** (mit etw) gehen, mitnehmen

to come in **38** *hier:* sich einschalten

to come through **50** durchkommen

to come to the table with sth **40** etw mitbringen

to come up against sth **118** auf etw stoßen

comfort **55** Behaglichkeit, Komfort

comfort break **55** kurze Pause

distance of comfort **106** Wohlfühl-abstand, Sicherheitsabstand

to become comfortable **21** sich wohl fühlen

command **16** Befehl

command **78** *hier:* Beherrschung, Beherr-schen

to commence **118** beginnen

commercial director **13** kaufmännische/r Leiter/in

commercial issues **91** Faktoren mit Be-zug auf Handel und Vertrieb

to commission **53** in Auftrag geben, beauftragen

commissioning **116** Inbetriebnahme, Ab-nahmetest

non-committal **113** unverbindlich

committed **114** engagiert

common **157** weit verbreitet, häufig

community **132** Gemeinschaft

company car **89** Geschäftswagen

comparable **80** vergleichbar

to compete **87** konkurrieren, kämpfen

competency **40** Kompetenz, Fähigkeit

complement **42** Ergänzung, Vervoll-ständigung

compliance **86** Befolgung, Einhaltung

in compliance with **36** gemäß

complimentary close **156** Grußformel, Schlussformel

to comply with sth **36** etw befolgen

composite **75** zusammengesetzt

compound **88** Mischung, Verbindung

comprehensive **83** umfassend, erschöpfend

compromise **88** Kompromiss

to compromise **89** sich einigen, einen Kompromiss schließen

compulsory **51** obligatorisch, Pflicht-

to whom it may concern **157** an die zu-ständige Abteilung

concession **89** Zugeständnis

concise **47** prägnant, knapp

to conclude sth from sth **67** etw aus etw schließen/ableiten

to draw a conclusion **133** einen Schluss ziehen

concrete **74** Beton

ready-mix concrete **75** Fertigbeton

condolence **170** Beileid, Kondolenz

conference call **6** Telefonkonferenz

confidence **43** Vertrauen, Selbstvertrauen

confident **78** selbstbewusst, selbstsicher

confidential **80** vertraulich, persönlich

to confront sb with sth **85** jmdn mit etw konfrontieren

congratulations **11** Gratulation, Glückwunsch

connection **34** Verbindung, Beziehung

consensus **55** Übereinstimmung, Einigung

to reach consensus **55** Übereinstimmung erzielen, sich einigen

to consider **88** berücksichtigen, erwägen, in Betracht ziehen

considerable **83** erheblich, beträchtlich

to consist of **66** bestehen aus

consistent **127** beständig

to consolidate **78** *Unternehmen etc.:* zusammenlegen

construction site **26** Baustelle

constructive **107** konstruktiv

consultancy **112** Beratungsbüro

mining consultant **78** Fachberater/in für den Bergbau

to consume **17** verbrauchen

consumer protection agency **130** Verbraucherschutzorganisation

time-consuming **17** zeitraubend

consumption **75** Verbrauch, Konsum

to make eye contact **101** Blickkontakt aufnehmen

to contaminate **50** verschmutzen, verunreinigen

content **104** Inhalt

contrary **16** Gegenteil, Gegensatz

on the contrary **16** im Gegenteil

to contribute **16** beitragen

contribution **40** Beitrag

in control **43** unter Kontrolle

conventional **69** herkömmlich, üblich

conventional wisdom **69** herrschende Meinung

to converse **125** sich unterhalten

to lose your cool *(coll.)* **73** die Fassung verlieren, sich aus der Ruhe bringen lassen

to cooperate **48** kooperieren

cooperative sourcing **94** Einkaufskooperation

to cope **125** zurechtkommen

hard copy **62** Ausdruck

extension cord **62** Verlängerungskabel

auto-correction **168** automatische Fehlerkorrektur

to correspond **169** entsprechen, übereinstimmen

correspondent **106** Briefschreiber/in

counterpart **13** Kollege, Kollegin

countryside **43** Landschaft, Natur

a couple of **22** ein paar

course of action **86** Vorgehen, Handlungsschritt

in the course of **161** im Laufe von

over the course of **38** im Verlauf von; im Laufe von; innerhalb von

to put the ball in sb's court **47** jmdm den Ball zuwerfen/zuspielen

to cover **38** abdecken

to cover for sb **158** für jmdn einspringen

It drives me crazy! **11** Das macht mich verrückt!

criteria **37** Kriterien

design criteria **114** Entwicklungskriterien

critical **28** kritisch, entscheidend

criticism **39** Kritik

to crowd around **50** sich drängen

crushed stone **75** Schotter

crystal **42** Kristall

culture clash **29** kultureller Gegensatz

curious **38** neugierig

curve **47** Kurve

to throw a curve ball **47** (mit einer Frage) überrumpeln

custom **28** Brauch, Gewohnheit, Sitte

custom **168** *hier:* Kundschaft

Customer technical support representative **6** Beauftragte/r für die technische Kundenbetreuung

CSR = customer service representative **51** Kundenberater/in

cut **53** Kürzung, Schnitt

D

damage **28** Schaden, Beschädigung

to damage **112** schädigen, beschädigen

dance **91** Tanz

data projector **38** Beamer

to date **39** bisher

to keep up to date **6** auf dem neuesten Stand halten

starting date **40** Einstellungsdatum

day-to-day **13** alltäglich

day job **120** Hauptberuf, Job

to daydream **54** mit offenen Augen träumen, tagträumen

it's early days **116** die Sache ist noch im Anfangsstadium; wir sind noch am Anfang

daytime **48** Tag

to entertain **6** unterhalten, einladen

business entertaining **6** Geschäfts-
veranstaltungen

enthusiasm **38** Begeisterung,
Enthusiasmus

to entitle sb to sth **52** jmdn zu etw
berechtigen

entrepreneur **68** Unternehmer/in

entry mode **66** Eintrittsstrategie für den
Markt

envious **100** neidisch

to envisage sth **118** etw voraussehen/
planen

equal **159** gleichberechtigt

to equip **38** ausstatten, ausrüsten

equipment **116** Anlage

loan equipment **48** Geräteverleih

lifting equipment **118** Hebevorrichtung,
Hubgerät

equivalent **40** Pendant, Äquivalent

ethos **42** Ethos

business etiquette **102** Geschäftsetikette

EMEA = Europe, Middle East, Africa **80**
Wirtschaftsraum Europa, Naher Osten,
Afrika

eve (= evening) **24** Abend

every now and then **38** hin und wieder,
gelegentlich

evidence **62** Beweis

to exceed **78** überschreiten, übertreffen

excess **68** Exzess, Übermaß

exchange **159** Austausch

excited **75** begeistert

to exclude **37** ausschließen

exclusivity **112** Exklusivität

Executive PA (= Executive Personal
Assistant) **6** Chefsekretär/in, persön-
liche/r Referent/in der Geschäftsführung

executive summary **39** Kurzdarstellung,
Zusammenfassung

executor **27** Nachlassverwalter/in,
Testamentsvollstrecker/in

to exhale **81** durchatmen, ausatmen

expansion **34** Expansion, Erweiterung

expectation **119** Erwartung

to expedite **118** beschleunigen

to experience **18** erleben

to explore **8** untersuchen, prüfen

to extend sth to sb **170** jmdm etw aus-
richten

extension cord **62** Verlängerungskabel

to a certain extent **167** bis zu einem
gewissen Grad, gewissermaßen

fire extinguisher **169** Feuerlöscher

to go the extra mile **88** keine Mühen
scheuen

to make eye contact **101** Blickkontakt
aufnehmen

to keep an eye on sb **130** ein Auge auf
jmdn haben, auf jmdn aufpassen

F

face-to-face **38** von Angesicht zu Angesicht, persönlich

to take sth at face value **111** etw für
bare Münze nehmen

to lose face **111** das Gesicht verlieren

poker-faced **85** mit unbewegter Miene

fairly **54** ziemlich, relativ

to fall asleep **54** einschlafen

to fall through **109** scheitern, nicht zu-
stande kommen

famous **26** berühmt

far off **37** fern, weit entfernt

by far **66** bei weitem

fascinated **100** fasziniert

fascinating **100** faszinierend

fatigue **72** Ermüdung

to favour sth **16** etw vorziehen

to be in favour of sth **51** für etw sein

to fax **39** faxen, per Fax senden

fear **43** Angst

feasibility **51** Machbarkeit, Durch-
führbarkeit

fed up **49** genervt

to **feel out of your depth** **14** überfordert
sein

to **feel part of** **43** sich als Teil fühlen

on **my feet** **84** aus dem Stegreif, in
schlagfertiger Art

field **26** Spielfeld, Platz

field visit **48** Vor-Ort-Termin, Kundenbesuch

file **15** Akte, Datei

to **fill** **38** *hier:* Stelle besetzen

to **fill in for sb** **13** für jmdn einspringen,
jmdn vertreten

to **fill sb in on sth** **53** jmdn über etw
informieren

filter **118** Filter

fine **86** Geldstrafe, Geldbuße

to **fine** **87** zu einer Geldstrafe verurteilen

That's fine with me. **37** In Ordnung.,
Einverstanden.

index finger **125** Zeigefinger

to **finish up** **86** enden

fire extinguisher **169** Feuerlöscher

at **first hand** **40** aus erster Hand

first-time **124** erstmalig, neu-

in **the first instance** **166** zunächst einmal

fist **42** Faust

to **see fit** **120** es für richtig halten,
es für angebracht halten

to **fix** **48** reparieren

flash drive **77** USB-Stick

flat washer **164** Unterlegscheibe

to **hit the floor** **50** auf den Boden fallen

flooring **88** Belag, Bodenbelag

flop **130** Reinfall

flour **165** Mehl

to **flow** **25** fließen, strömen

flow chart **74** Flussdiagramm

to **go with the flow** **68** mit dem Strom
schwimmen

to **have a flutter on** *(coll.)* **42** *Wette:* sein
Glück versuchen

follow-on **159** Folge-

Do you follow me? **37** Können Sie mir
folgen?, Verstehen Sie?

following **126** nach

to **shoot yourself in the foot** **73** sich ins
eigene Fleisch schneiden

carbon footprint **66** CO_2-Bilanz

for **22** seit

for sure *(coll.)* **134** ganz sicher, ganz
bestimmt

task force **51** Arbeitsgruppe

to **forecast** **112** voraussagen, vorhersagen

forensic **160** forensisch, gerichts-

forest **117** Wald

starter application form **156** Erstantrag

formality **17** Formalität, Förmlichkeit

forum **55** Forum

forward **132** Voraus-

to **move forward** **39** vorankommen

to **put forward** **38** vorschlagen, vortragen

to **foster** **16** fördern, verstärken

lost and found department **80** Fundbüro

to **lay a foundation** **106** eine Grundlage
schaffen

founding **16** Gründung

fragrance **126** Duft, Parfum

time frame **115** zeitlicher Rahmen

franchisee **65** Lizenznehmer/in

franchiser **65** Lizenzgeber/in

frankly **25** offen, ehrlich gesagt

frankness **111** Offenheit, Unbefangenheit

to **freak out** **43** ausflippen

freebie **130** Werbegeschenk

freedom **120** Freiheit

up front *(coll.)* **120** im Voraus

frown **64** Stirnrunzeln

to **frown** **85** die Stirn runzeln

fungal **88** Pilz-

furious **100** wütend

to **further** **132** fördern

G

to **gain access** **88** Zugang erhalten

to **gamble** **42** spielen, wetten

to **keep to sth** **38** sich an etw halten

to **keep track of sth** **72** den Überblick über etw behalten

to **keep up** **6** mithalten

to **keep up to date** **6** auf dem neuesten Stand halten

to **keep your mouth shut** *(coll.)* **69** den Mund halten

key point **38** springender Punkt, Schwerpunkt

keynote **10** Leitgedanke

keynote speech **10** Eröffnungsrede

to **kick one's ass** *(coll.)* **69** jmdm in den Hintern treten

to **kill two birds with one stone** **130** zwei Fliegen mit einer Klappe schlagen

one of a kind **127** einzigartig, einmalig

kitchen top **88** Küchenarbeitsplatte

knee **50** Knie

GTKY = Getting to know you **74** Kennenlern-

working knowledge **40** Grundkenntnisse

knowledgeable **127** kompetent, versiert

well-known **41** bekannt

L

lack **75** Mangel

sb lacks sth **106** jmdm fehlt/mangelt es an etw

ladder **16** Leiter

lap **50** Schoß

large screen **42** Großbildschirm, Großbildleinwand

large-scale **114** groß angelegt, in großem Maßstab

laser **48** Laser

to **last** **66** dauern

last-minute **130** in letzter Minute, kurzfristig

lately **49** in letzter Zeit

lateness **86** Verspätung

later on **10** später

latest **6** neueste/r/s

lattice **16** Gitter

to **launch an attack at sb** **55** einen Angriff auf jmdn starten

to **lay** **116** verlegen

layered **16** geschichtet

to **lay a foundation** **106** eine Grundlage schaffen

to **lay off** **76** entlassen

to **lay out sth** **42** gestalten, auslegen

lead time **15** Herstellungszeit

to **lead in** **38** einleiten

to **lead to** **49** *hier:* führen zu

lean **8** schlank, verschlankt

to **learn the ropes** *(coll.)* **38** sich einarbeiten, die Basics

to **leave open** **90** offenlassen, offenhalten

to **leave out** **104** auslassen

leisurely **99** geruhsam, gemütlich

lengthy **106** übermäßig lang, langatmig

let alone **13** geschweige denn

body of letter **156** Hauptteil eines Briefes

capital letter **157** Großbuchstabe

letterhead **156** Briefkopf

liable **87** haftbar

to **liaise** **13** zusammenarbeiten

lift **119** Mitfahrgelegenheit

lifting equipment **118** Hebevorrichtung, Hubgerät

in light of **90** angesichts

likewise **84** ebenso, gleichfalls

limestone **75** Kalkstein

time limit **38** Zeitvorgabe, zeitlicher Rahmen

limited access **58** beschränkter Zugang

to **limp** **50** hinken, humpeln

line **138** *hier:* Branche

in line with **39** im Rahmen, in Übereinstimmung mit

bottom line **89** Fazit, das Entscheidende

lines of reporting **13** Kommunikationskette, Ablauf

trade link **12** Handelsverbindung

linking word **50** Verbindungswort

shopping list **54** Einkaufsliste

literally **111** wörtlich, buchstäblich

to go live **22** online gehen

standard of living **78** Lebensstandard

loan equipment **48** Geräteverleih

in the long run **66** auf lange Sicht, auf die Dauer

long-lasting **94** dauerhaft, anhaltend

to look into sth **24** etw untersuchen, etw prüfen

to look at sth **92** etw in Betracht ziehen

to lose your cool *(coll.)* **73** die Fassung verlieren, sich aus der Ruhe bringen lassen

to lose face **111** das Gesicht verlieren

lost and found department **80** Fundbüro

lovely **35** schön, herrlich

to try one's luck **42** sein Glück versuchen

lucrative **96** lukrativ, einträglich

M

imaging machine **48** MRT-Gerät, Röntgengerät

tailor-made **48** zugeschnitten, passgenau

maintenance **48** Instandhaltung, Wartung

to make eye contact **101** Blickkontakt aufnehmen

to make the plane **81** den Flieger bekommen

to make reference to **139** Bezug nehmen auf

Did I make myself clear? **38** Haben Sie mich verstanden?, Habe ich mich verständlich ausgedrückt?

decision-maker **10** Entscheidungsträger/in

to malfunction **48** nicht richtig funktionieren

inventory management **17** Lagerverwaltung

value management **127** Wertmanagement

area sales manager **13** Gebietsverkaufsleiter/in

regional sales manager **13** regionale/r Verkaufsleiter/in

business unit manager **15** Leiter/in des Geschäftsbereichs

mansion **68** Villa, herrschaftlicher Wohnsitz

manual **6** Handbuch

manual **49** handgeschrieben, handschriftlich

to map out **76** festlegen, vorlegen, aufzeigen

margin **88** Spielraum

profit margin **88** Gewinnspanne

market economy **75** Marktwirtschaft

match **93** Gegenstück

matrix **13** Gerüst, Netz, Matrix

MD (= Managing Director) **13** Geschäftsführer/in

mealtime **102** Essenszeit

to mean to do sth **26** etw tun wollen, etw vorhaben

meantime **39** Zwischenzeit

measurable **55** messbar, merklich

measure **80** Maß, Maßstab

to measure **131** messen

social media **34** soziale Medien, soziale Netzwerke

medium-term **36** mittelfristig

sales meeting **34** Vertriebsveranstaltung

to memorize **79** auswendig lernen, sich einprägen

mental **81** geistig

mentality **17** Mentalität

to mess up **60** vermasseln, verpatzen

to get a message across **62** eine Aussage vermitteln

methodology **132** Methodologie, Methodik

mic = microphone **64** Mikrofon

to micromanage **120** sich in Details einmischen

micro-organism **114** Mikroorganismus

EMEA = Europe, Middle East, Africa **80** Wirtschaftsraum Europa, Naher Osten, Afrika

mildly **59** ein wenig, etwas

to **go the extra mile** **88** keine Mühen scheuen

milestone **29** Meilenstein

to **have sb in mind** **37** an jmdn denken

bear in mind **92** denken Sie daran, vergessen Sie nicht

miner **14** Bergarbeiter/in

mineral **75** Mineral

mining consultant **78** Fachberater/in für den Bergbau

minor **22** klein, gering

last-minute **130** in letzter Minute, kurzfristig

a minute's walk **26** ein Katzensprung

to **misplace** **80** verlegen

misprint **168** Fehldruck

to **miss** **170** vermissen

to **go missing** **80** verloren gehen

mist **129** Nebel, Dunst

by mistake **50** aus Versehen

to **mistake sth for sth** **69** etw für etw halten, etw mit etw verwechseln

misunderstanding **50** Missverständnis, Meinungsverschiedenheit

to **mix** **88** mischen

mix-up **109** Durcheinander, Missverständnis

ready-mix concrete **75** Fertigbeton

mixture **13** Mischung

mobile **43** mobil

entry mode **66** Eintrittsstrategie für den Markt

modification **137** Änderung, Modifikation

modifier **83** Modifikator

to **modify** **128** verändern

to **monitor** **109** überwachen, kontrollieren

mood **62** Stimmung, Laune

to **mop** **50** wischen

motorized **42** motorisiert

motorway **109** Autobahn

to **keep your mouth shut** *(coll.)* **69** den Mund halten

move **37** Schritt

to **move forward** **39** vorankommen

to **move on** **38** weitermachen, fortfahren

to **multiply** **162** vervielfachen

municipal **116** Gemeinde-, Stadt-, städtisch

mural **42** Wandgemälde

musician **68** Musiker/in

must-have **89** ein Muss

to **mute** **37** (ein Gerät) auf „stumm" schalten

My pleasure. **26** Gern., Mit Vergnügen.

N

nail **67** Nagel

namely **72** nämlich, und zwar

narrow **92** schmal, beschränkt

nationwide **57** landesweit

nature **119** Art, Wesen

to **navigate** **51** navigieren, bedienen

to **near** **118** sich nähern

nearby **24** nahe gelegen

need **132** Bedarf

negotiating table **110** Verhandlungstisch

negotiator **102** Unterhändler/in

nephew **26** Neffe

newborn **95** gerade geboren

newborn **120** Neugeborenes

niece **26** Nichte

nightmare **81** Albtraum

to **get down to the nitty-gritty** *(coll.)* **73** zur Sache kommen

Nobel Prize **128** Nobelpreis

to **nod** **130** nicken

noise **26** Lärm, Geräusch

polite noise **131** höfliche Bemerkung

non-tactile **106** berührungsarm, berührungslos

non-aerosol **130** aerosolfrei

noticeable **80** deutlich, auffällig

now and again **115** hin und wieder

every now and then **38** hin und wieder, gelegentlich

No way! **59** Auf keinen Fall!

nozzle **118** Düse

nuisance **11** Ärger

a number of times **102** mehrfach, mehrmals

numerous **132** zahlreich

dome nut **164** Hutmutter

half nut **164** halbe Mutter

O

objection **88** Einwand

obligation **27** Verpflichtung, Pflicht

observation **107** Beobachtung

obstacle **53** Hindernis, Schwierigkeit

occasion **51** Gelegenheit, Anlass, Ereignis

occasionally **54** gelegentlich, hin und wieder

to let sb off the hook **105** jmdm aus der Klemme helfen

brush-off **59** Absage

to offend **129** beleidigen

Chief Information Officer (= CIO) **6** Leiter/in der Abteilung Informationstechnologie

to okay **101** genehmigen

old town **26** Altstadt

on **168** bei

once in a while **95** von Zeit zu Zeit

at once **49** sofort

one of a kind **127** einzigartig, einmalig

one-to-one **129** von Angesicht zu Angesicht, persönlich

on hand **125** bereit, zur Verfügung

on my feet **84** aus dem Stegreif, in schlagfertiger Art

on receipt **163** bei Erhalt

to leave open **90** offenlassen, offenhalten

opening **47** erste/r/s, einleitend

opening **47** Eröffnungs-

operational **94** betrieblich, Einsatz-, betriebsbereit

retail operator **36** Einzelhändler/in

as opposed to **162** im Gegensatz zu

optional **29** freiwillig, fakultativ

oral **40** mündlich

sales order processing **15** Auftragsabwicklung

in working order **39** in betriebsfähigem Zustand

organigram **84** Organigramm

ought to **52** sollen

out of action **26** außer Gefecht

That's out of the question. **59** Das kommt nicht in Frage.

out of office reply **158** Abwesenheitsnachricht/-notiz

to run out of sth **62** etw nicht mehr haben

outcome **86** Ergebnis, Resultat

outdated **49** veraltet, nicht mehr aktuell

outgoing shipment **87** Warenversand

retail outlet **40** Einzelhandelsgeschäft, Ladengeschäft

outline **63** Übersicht

outside **81** außerhalb

outside **95** *hier:* draußen, nach draußen

to outsource **53** ausgliedern, auslagern

outsourcing **53** Ausgliederung, Auslagerung

outstanding **166** ausstehend

to outweigh **133** überwiegen

over the course of **38** im Verlauf von, im Lauf von, innerhalb von

overdue **122** überfällig

to overlap **91** sich überschneiden

to oversee **116** überwachen, beaufsichtigen

to oversimplify **106** zu stark vereinfachen

to overwhelm **73** überwältigen, überschütten

state-owned **75** staatlich, Staats-

owner **81** Besitzer/in

P

Executive PA (= Executive Personal Assistant) **6** Chefsekretär/in, persönliche/r Referent/in der Geschäftsführung

pace **62** Tempo, Geschwindigkeit

to pace **67** das Tempo bestimmen

parallel **38** parallel

in parallel **38** parallel dazu
parameter **94** Parameter
to set the parameters **94** den Rahmen
setzen
to paraphrase **47** anders ausdrücken,
umschreiben
Pardon? **38** Wie bitte?
to beg sb's pardon **125** jmdn um
Verzeihung bitten
Parmesan **42** Parmesan
to feel part of **43** sich als Teil fühlen
partial **51** teilweise, partiell
to participate **38** teilnehmen
participation **85** Teilnahme, Beteiligung
particularly **34** insbesondere, vor allem
to pass sth **112** etw bestehen
to pass on **38** weitergeben
to pass sb **102** an jmdm vorbeigehen
passionate **127** leidenschaftlich
patch *(coll.)* **120** *hier:* Phase
path **68** Weg, Pfad
patient **79** geduldig
to pause **47** pausieren, innehalten
to pay attention **50** aufpassen, aufmerksam sein
to pay a visit **50** einen Besuch abstatten
to pay out **68** auszahlen
payment system **40** Zahlungssystem
payment gateway **40** Zahlungsportal
peak **72** Höhepunkt
peer **132** Fachkollege, Fachkollegin
per cent **38** Prozent
to perceive **100** wahrnehmen, annehmen
perception **51** Wahrnehmung, Verständnis
to perform **15** ausführen, vollziehen, er-
füllen
performance rating **49** Leistungsbe-
wertung
sales performance **126** Verkaufsergebnis,
Absatz
permit **72** Genehmigung, Erlaubnis
persistent **67** beharrlich, hartnäckig
perspective **40** Perspektive, Blickwinkel

to put into perspective **75** relativieren
phosphoric acid **88** Phosphorsäure
set phrase **38** Floskel, Formel
turn of phrase **73** Ausdrucksweise
physical **40** materiell, stofflich
to pick up sth **40** sich etw aneignen
picky **120** wählerisch, pingelig
pie **7** Torte
pie chart **7** Tortendiagramm
pilot project **128** Pilotprojekt, Modellver-
such
pipe **11** Rohr, Leitung
to pitch **73** vortragen
in place **80** etabliert
to place trust in sb **106** zu jmdm Vertrauen haben, an jmdn glauben
to plan in **26** einplanen
action plan **38** Maßnahmenplan
to make the plane **81** den Flieger bekommen
water treatment plant **9** Wasseraufbereitungsanlage, Kläranlage
plate **29** Teller
to play a role **100** eine Rolle spielen
to play for time **93** Zeit gewinnen,
Zeit schinden
to play sports **138** Sport treiben
player **94** Akteur/in
pleasure **26** Vergnügen, Freude, Spaß
My pleasure. **26** Gern., Mit Vergnügen.
adaptor plug **62** Adapterstecker
to plummet **75** stürzen, absacken
pocket-sized **129** im Taschenformat
point of sale **36** Verkaufsstelle
point of sale terminal **40** Kasse
to point out **92** betonen, hervorheben
there's no point in **112** es hat keinen
Zweck, ...
key point **38** springender Punkt,
Schwerpunkt
up to a point **51** bis zu einem bestimmten
Punkt
bullet point **63** Aufzählungszeichen

bottleneck point **78** Engpass, Engstelle
poker-faced **85** mit unbewegter Miene
polite noise **131** höfliche Bemerkung
politeness **29** Höflichkeit
poll **126** Umfrage
to pop in *(coll.)* **120** vorbeischauen
sparsly populated **75** dünn besiedelt
possibility **37** Möglichkeit
post-production **104** Nachbearbeitung
postage **163** Porto
to keep sb posted **133** jmdn auf dem
Laufenden halten
pouring rain **81** strömender Regen
power supply **58** Elektrizitätsversorgung,
Stromversorgung
practice **40** Vorgehensweise, Praxis
best practice **132** optimales Vorgehen,
vorbildliches Verfahren
precise **15** präzise, genau
predefined **132** im Voraus bestimmt/fest-
gelegt
predetermined **16** im Voraus bestimmt
to pre-install **81** vorinstallieren
present **37** anwesend
press release **157** Pressemitteilung,
Presseerklärung
to prevent **28** verhindern
preventative **48** Präventiv-, vorbeugend
preventative check **48** Wartung
prevention **48** Vorbeugung, Schutz
sneak preview **104** Vorpremiere
pricing **88** Preis
primitive **57** primitiv
principle **67** Prinzip
in principle **93** im Prinzip
in print **101** gedruckt
printed circuit board **86** Leiterplatte,
Platine
prior **37** früher, vorherig
to prioritize **40** Prioritäten setzen, der
Wichtigkeit nach ordnen
to privatize **75** privatisieren
prize **43** Preis

Nobel Prize **128** Nobelpreis
probable **101** wahrscheinlich
to run into problems **51** Probleme
bekommen
proceeds **68** Erlös
sales order processing **15** Auftragsabwicklung
to procure **78** beschaffen
procurement **13** Beschaffung
procurement department **94** Einkaufs-
abteilung
head of production **13** Produktionsleiter/in
productive **38** ergebnisreich, produktiv
profile **126** Image
profit margin **88** Gewinnspanne
profitable **82** gewinnbringend, einträglich
programmer **68** Programmierer/in
progress report **39** Lagebericht, Zwischenbericht
in progress **116** im Gange
to progress **161** vorankommen, Fortschritte
machen
data projector **38** Beamer
promotion **11** Aufstieg, Beförderung
promotion **130** *hier:* Werbung, Werbeaktion
prompt **48** prompt, unverzüglich
prompt **71** Stichwort
proof **69** Beweis
proper **43** richtig, anständig
request for proposal (RFP) **94** (kom-
plexere) Ausschreibung
props **67** Requisiten, *hier:* Gegenstand
prospect **40** Aussicht
protection **130** Schutz
consumer protection agency **130** Verbraucherschutzorganisation
to prove to be sth **39** sich als etw
erweisen
to prove **69** beweisen
proverb **41** Sprichwort
training provider **37** Anbieter von Weiterbildungen
service provider **40** Dienstleister

provocative **131** provozierend

psychology **69** Psychologie

public transport **38** öffentliche Verkehrs-
mittel

publicity **138** Werbung, Publicity

purification **116** Reinigung

to purify **116** reinigen

on purpose **112** absichtlich, mit Absicht

pushy **60** ehrgeizig, fordernd

to put at risk **80** einem Risiko aussetzen,
gefährden

to put forward **38** vorschlagen, vortragen

to put into perspective **75** relativieren

to put sb at ease **137** jmdm seine Befan-
genheit nehmen

to put the ball in sb's court **47** jmdm
den Ball zuwerfen/zuspielen

puzzle **43** Rätsel, Puzzle

puzzling **100** rätselhaft

Q

to be of bad quality **39** von schlechter
Qualität sein

Q&A = question and answer **83** Frage
und Antwort

That's out of the question. **59** Das kommt
nicht in Frage.

closed question **103** Entscheidungsfrage

questioner **129** Fragesteller/in

to take questions **66** Fragen beantworten

to quit **14** kündigen, aussteigen

to quit **69** *hier:* aufhören

quite a bit **35** ziemlich viel

to quote **74** zitieren

quote *(coll.)* **130** Zitat

R

pouring rain **81** strömender Regen

to raise **81** heben, erhöhen

to raise **133** *hier:* zur Sprache bringen,
erwähnen

to rank **16** einstufen

ranking **16** Einstufung

rate **23** Rate, Quote

traffic rate **23** Zugriffsquote

growth rate **133** Wachstumsrate

performance rating **49** Leistungs-
bewertung

re-engineered **17** neustrukturiert,
überarbeitet

to reach a decision **51** zu einer
Entscheidung kommen, entschließen

to reach capacity **38** mit voller Leistung
arbeiten

to reach consensus **55** Übereinstimmung
erzielen, sich einigen

to read up on sth **88** sich über etw
informieren, etw recherchieren

to readjust **48** neu einstellen, nachstellen

ready-mix concrete **75** Fertigbeton

real time **67** Echtzeit

rebranding **129** ein neues Markenimage
geben, einen neuen Markennamen geben

to rebuild **116** wieder aufbauen

to recall **80** *Produkt:* zurückrufen

to recap **65** rekapitulieren, zusammenfassen

receipt **49** Quittung

on receipt **163** bei Erhalt

recently **13** kürzlich, neulich

recession **16** Rezession

recipient **156** Empfänger/in

to reclaim **80** zurückverlangen, abholen

brand recognition **129** Wiedererkennung
einer Marke, Markenbewusstsein

to recognize **102** anerkennen,
hier: einhalten

to reconsider **88** noch einmal über-
denken

to record **53** dokumentieren, aufzeichnen

record **136** Rekord

recording **11** Aufzeichnung

to recover **26** sich erholen

to recover **81** *hier:* wiedererlangen,
zurückbekommen, wiederherstellen

recovery **80** Wiederbeschaffung, Wieder-
erlangung

recruit **76** Neuzugang
recruitment **13** Anwerbung, Einstellung
recruitment drive **38** Einstellungs-
verfahren
recycler **14** Entsorger, Recycler
to redo **105** noch einmal tun, neu machen
reduction **138** Reduktion, Verminderung
with reference to **22** mit Bezug auf,
bezüglich
terms of reference **129** *hier:* Referenz,
Bezug, Hintergrundinformation
to make reference to **139** Bezug nehmen
auf
to reflect **170** spiegeln, reflektieren
refusal **59** Ablehnung, Absage,
Verweigerung
to regain **75** wiedergewinnen
in regard to **87** in Bezug auf
Re = regarding **160** Betreff, betreffend
regardless of **53** ungeachtet, ohne
Rücksicht auf
regional sales manager **13** regionale/r
Verkaufsleiter/in
to register **81** registrieren
cash register **37** Kasse
regret **170** Bedauern
regulatory **86** Aufsichts-
regulatory board **86** Aufsichtsrat, Aufsichtsgremium
to rehearse **62** proben, sich leise vorsagen
rejection **59** Ablehnung, Zurückweisung
relative **38** Verwandte/r
relative **75** verhältnismäßig, relativ
release **136** Herausbringen, Neu-
erscheinung
press release **157** Pressemitteilung,
Presseerklärung
to relocate **90** umsiedeln, den Standort
verlegen
reluctant **85** zögerlich
to rely on sth **62** auf etw vertrauen
That remains to be seen. **92** Das bleibt
abzuwarten.

reminder **155** Erinnerung, Mahnung
remotely **51** entfernt, im Geringsten
remotely **81** *hier:* fern-, von Ferne
to renovate **138** renovieren
reorganization **11** Umorganisation, Neu-
organisation
rep = representative **139** Vertreter/in
repeated **78** wiederholt
replacement **160** Ersatz, Auswechseln
out of office reply **158** Abwesenheits-
nachricht/-notiz
progress report **39** Lagebericht,
Zwischenbericht
lines of reporting **13** Kommunikationskette, Ablauf
Customer technical support
representative **6** Beauftragte/r für die
technische Kundenbetreuung
CSR = customer service
representative **51** Kundenberater/in
request for proposal (RFP) **94** (kom-
plexere) Ausschreibung
to do research into sth **102** etw näher
untersuchen
with no reservation **92** ohne Vorbehalt
reserved **85** zurückhaltend, reserviert
to resolve **167** lösen, klären
to respect **51** respektieren, achten
budgetary restriction **161** Haushalts-
einsparungen, Sparmaßnahmen
to result in **17** führen zu
retail operator **36** Einzelhändler/in
retail staff **38** Verkaufspersonal
retail outlet **40** Einzelhandelsgeschäft,
Ladengeschäft
to retrieve **81** zurückholen
in return for **65** als Gegenleistung für
return **158** Rückkehr
to reveal **81** erkennen lassen, zeigen
reverse auction **86** Ausschreibung,
Auftragsauktion
to review **8** durchsehen, prüfen
reward **51** Belohnung

to **get rid of** 17 loswerden
rigid 16 starr, unflexibel
to **ring a bell** *(coll.)* 37 bekannt vorkommen
rise 105 Anstieg, Zunahme
to **put at risk** 80 einem Risiko aussetzen, gefährden
to **carry a risk** 84 ein Risiko bergen, risikobehaftet sein
robot 18 Roboter
robotic 117 Roboter-
robotics 72 Robotertechnik, Robotik
rock 116 Gestein, Fels
threaded rod 164 Gewindestange
to **play a role** 100 eine Rolle spielen
rolling start 38 Start aus einem fortlaufenden Projekt
rope 38 Seil, Tau
to **learn the ropes** *(coll.)* 38 sich einarbeiten, die Basics lernen
rough 63 grob
roughly 75 ungefähr, grob
roulette wheel 42 Roulette
round 112 Runde
row 78 Reihe
rubber 119 Gummi
rude 49 unhöflich
to **run** 13 leiten
to **run into problems** 51 Probleme bekommen
to **run out of sth** 62 etw nicht mehr haben
to **run over schedule** 117 den Zeitplan nicht einhalten, im Verzug sein
in the long run 66 auf lange Sicht, auf die Dauer
up and running 37 in Gang, funktionierend
to **rush** 80 eilen, hetzen

S

sacred 27 heilig
sad 170 traurig

sadly 102 leider, bedauerlicherweise
easier said than done 130 leichter gesagt als getan
salary increase 89 Lohnerhöhung
point of sale 36 Verkaufsstelle
point of sale terminal 40 Kasse
sales meeting 34 Vertriebsveranstaltung
sales order processing 15 Auftragsabwicklung
sales performance 126 Verkaufsergebnis, Absatz
sales training 13 Verkaufstraining
area sales manager 13 Gebietsverkaufsleiter/in
regional sales manager 13 regionale/r Verkaufsleiter/in
salutation 167 Begrüßung, Anrede
sarcasm 106 Sarkasmus
sarcastic 101 sarkastisch
savvy *(coll.)* 111 schlau, kompetent
saying 41 Redensart
large-scale 114 groß angelegt, in großem Maßstab
scandal 42 Skandal, Klatsch
worst case scenario 77 der schlimmste Fall, größter anzunehmender Unfall – GAU
scene 34 Szene
scenery 35 Landschaft
scent 126 Duft, Parfum
sceptical 90 skeptisch
to **run over schedule** 117 den Zeitplan nicht einhalten, im Verzug sein
scope 37 Bereich, Umfang, Rahmen
to **be beyond the scope of sth** 37 außerhalb des Rahmens von etw liegen, den Rahmen von etw sprengen
to **score** 37 Punkte erzielen
to **screen** 81 untersuchen, überprüfen
large screen 42 Großbildschirm, Großbildleinwand
script 42 Drehbuch
back seat 81 Rücksitz, Rückbank
seating 62 Platz, Sitzfläche

secondment **9** vorübergehende Versetzung

to **be on secondment 9** vorübergehend versetzt sein

secrecy 106 Geheimhaltung, Verschwiegenheit

security checkpoint 80 Sicherheitskontrolle

to **see fit 120** es für richtig/angebracht halten

That remains to be seen. **92** Das bleibt abzuwarten.

seldom 155 selten

self-serve buffet 104 Selbstbedienungsbuffet

hard sell 107 aggressive Strategie, aggressive Verkaufstaktik

best-selling 106 häufig verkauft, meistverkauft

to **send one's apologies 37** sich entschuldigen lassen

to **send off 38** wegschicken

to **send out 94** verschicken

sender 156 Absender/in

sensitive 80 empfindlich, sensibel

sensitivity 28 Einfühlungsvermögen

sequencing word 15 Gliederungswort

serial 94 Serien-, Fortsetzungs-

to **serve as a stepping stone 59** als Brücke dienen

service 8 Kundenbetreuung

service provider 40 Dienstleister

CSR = customer service representative 51 Kundenberater/in

business services IT 128 IT-Dienstleister

session 13 Treffen, Termin

set 38 *hier:* fertig, bereit

set phrase 38 Floskel, Formel

to **set a goal 75** ein Ziel setzen

to **set aside 132** zur Seite legen, einplanen

to **set the parameters 94** den Rahmen setzen

to **set up 37** errichten

skill set 40 Anforderungsprofil

setback 118 Rückschlag

setting up 36 das Einrichten

in a social setting 102 in Gesellschaft

to **settle 166** ausgleichen, bezahlen

settlement 166 Ausgleich, Bezahlung

ship 80 Schiff

to **shock 81** schocken, erschüttern

to **shoot yourself in the foot** *(coll.)* **73** sich ins eigene Fleisch schneiden

shooter 25 Schütze, Schützin

shopping list 54 Einkaufsliste

short break 26 Kurzurlaub

to **keep short 24** knapp halten, kurz halten

shortlist 112 Auswahlliste

shortly 169 in Kürze, bald

to **shout 38** schreien, brüllen

to **show up 49** auftauchen, erscheinen

trade show 34 Handelsmesse

to **shut down 78** schließen

to **keep your mouth shut** *(coll.)* **69** den Mund halten

shy 101 schüchtern, scheu

to **signpost 67** schildern, ausschildern

silence 47 Stille

simulation 28 Vortäuschung

to **sink 78** sinken, absinken

site 26 Stelle, Platz

construction site 26 Baustelle

greenfield site 117 nicht erschlossenes Baugrundstück, grüne Wiese

pocket-sized 129 im Taschenformat

skill set 40 Anforderungsprofil

to **slip 50** ausrutschen

to **slip sth in 21** etw einfließen lassen

to **slow down 26** verlangsamen

to **slump 78** fallen, sinken

to **smell 102** riechen

smoker 52 Raucher/in

to **smuggle 78** schmuggeln

smuggling 78 Schmuggel, Schmuggeln

snake 102 Schlange

snapshot **114** Kurzdarstellung
sneak preview **104** Vorpremiere
soaked **81** durchnässt
to soar **75** in die Höhe schnellen, an-
steigen
sociable **102** gesellig
social butterfly **25** Partygänger/in
social media **34** soziale Medien,
soziale Netzwerke
in a social setting **102** in Gesellschaft
somewhat **75** etwas, ziemlich
sort of (coll.) **13** irgendwie
sound **48** solide, vernünftig, fest
to source **15** beziehen
source **66** Quelle
sparse **75** spärlich
sparsly populated **75** dünn besiedelt
to speak up **37** lauter sprechen
speaking of **25** apropos
specialist **42** Spezial-, Fach-
speciality ingredients **88** Spezial-
rohstoffe
specifically **34** speziell, besonders
spectrum **59** Spektrum
to speculate **100** spekulieren, Vermutun-
gen anstellen
keynote speech **10** Eröffnungsrede
speedboat **42** Motorboot, Schnellboot
to spend **26** verbringen
to spend **163** hier: ausgeben
sponsor **138** Sponsor
sponsorship **126** finanzielle Förderung
to play sports **138** Sport treiben
hot spot **66** interessanter Ort
springtime **25** Frühling
spy **138** Spion
to squeeze **112** unter Druck setzen
stability **112** Stabilität
stack **42** Haufen, Stapel
retail staff **38** Verkaufspersonal
to stagnate **85** stagnieren
stainless **164** rostfrei
stainless steel **94** Edelstahl

to stall **99** zum Stillstand kommen, ins
Stocken geraten
to stand **88** stehen, hoch sein
to stand by **48** zur Verfügung stehen,
bereitstehen
to stand in for sb **50** für jmdn einspringen
standard of living **78** Lebensstandard
standing **169** Rang, Ansehen
stare **85** Starren
to start **68** gründen, aufmachen
rolling start **38** aus einem fortlaufenden
Projekt startend
starter application form **156** Erstantrag
starting date **40** Einstellungsdatum
to starve **86** hungern, verhungern
to be starving (coll.) **86** einen Wahnsinns-
hunger haben
state-owned **75** staatlich, Staats-
to steal **77** stehlen
stepping stone **59** Trittstein, Sprungbrett
to stick to sth **106** an etw festhalten,
bei etw bleiben
to stick up **67** in die Höhe stehen,
herausstehen
sticker **81** Aufkleber
stiff **17** steif
stock **42** Aktie
crushed stone **75** Schotter
to kill two birds with one stone **130**
zwei Fliegen mit einer Klappe schlagen
storage cabinet **30** Lagerschrank,
Datenschutzschrank
storyboard **104** Storyboard, Ablaufplan
straight **25** offen, direkt, unverblümt
straight shooter **25** jemand, der sehr
direkt ist
strategic **74** strategisch
strategy **34** Strategie
to streamline **15** rationalisieren, beschleunigen
to strike **53** schlagen, treffen
to strike sb as **137** jmdm als ... vorkommen
to strike up sth **10** etw beginnen

Strike while the iron's hot. 53 Man muss das Eisen schmieden, solange es heiß ist.

to **struggle 88** sich schwertun, sich abmühen

case study 28 Fallstudie

stunning 100 fantastisch, umwerfend

stupid 81 dumm, blöd

subcontractor 37 Subunternehmer/in

to **submit 15** einreichen

subscription fee 81 Mitgliedsbeitrag

to **substitute 50** ersetzen, vertreten

substitute 51 Ersatz

substitution 69 Ersatz

successful 38 erfolgreich

succinct 73 kurz und treffend, prägnant

suit 13 Anzug

executive summary 39 Kurzdarstellung, Zusammenfassung

in **summary 130** zusammenfassend

sub-supplier 130 Zulieferer, Sublieferant

supply 48 Mittel

supply 78 *hier:* Angebot, Vorrat

power supply 58 Elektrizitätsversorgung, Stromversorgung

to **support 38** unterstützen

Customer technical support representative 6 Beauftragte/r für die technische Kundenbetreuung

diagnostic support 48 Hilfe bei der Fehlersuche; Fehleranalyse

supportive 40 hilfreich, unterstützend

for sure *(coll.)* **134** ganz sicher, ganz bestimmt

surprised 100 überrascht, verwundert

suspense 127 Spannung

to **keep sb in suspense 127** jmdn auf die Folter spannen

swift 67 schnell, rasch

to **swing 43** schwingen, baumeln

SWOT analysis (SWOT = Strengths, Weaknesses, Opportunities and Threats) 34 Stärken-Schwächen-Analyse

sympathy 50 Verständnis, Mitgefühl, Unterstützung

payment system 40 Zahlungssystem

T

to **come to the table with 40** etw mitbringen

negotiating table 110 Verhandlungstisch

tact 115 Taktgefühl

non-tactile 106 berührungsarm, berührungslos

tailor 48 Schneider/in

tailor-made 48 zugeschnitten, passgenau

to **take a while 6** eine Weile dauern

to **take care of sth 105** sich um etw kümmern

to **take in 85** begreifen

to **take it in turns 38** sich abwechseln

to **take on 104** annehmen

to **take questions 66** Fragen beantworten

to **take sth at face value 111** etw für bare Münze nehmen

to **take up 49** beanspruchen

to **talk business 109** Geschäfte machen, über Geschäftliches sprechen

tall 13 hoch

task force 51 Arbeitsgruppe

tasty 26 lecker, schmackhaft

tax 78 Steuer

team-building 42 Teamentwicklung

technical writer 101 technische/r Redakteur/in

to **tell time 131** die Uhr lesen

How can you tell? 22 Woher wissen Sie das?

to **tempt sb 69** in Versuchung führen

temptation 69 Versuchung, Verlockung

to **tend to sth 43** zu etw neigen, zu etw tendieren

to **tender 36** ein Angebot einreichen

tender 36 Angebot

call for tenders 36 Ausschreibung

invitation to tender 36 Ausschreibung (Preis)

tension **57** Anspannung, Spannung
tentative **51** zaghaft, zögernd
medium-term **36** mittelfristig
point of sale terminal **40** Kasse
in terms of **28** im Sinne von

terms of reference **129** *hier:* Referenz,
Bezug, Hintergrundinformation
to test the waters **111** die Lage ausloten
testimonial **48** Kundenbewertung, Testimonial
That's fine with me. **37** In Ordnung.,
Einverstanden.
theft **81** Diebstahl
themed **42** Themen-, themenorientiert
every now and then **38** hin und wieder,
gelegentlich
There are too many chiefs and not
enough Indians. *(coll.)* **13** Es gibt zu
viele Leute, die Befehle erteilen, und nicht
genug Leute, die die Arbeit machen.
thief **81** Dieb/in
to think up **38** sich ausdenken, erfinden
to think ahead **81** vorausdenken,
vorausplanen
it is thought to **56** es wurde entschieden;
man denkt, dass
thoughtful **67** gut durchdacht, wohl
überlegt
to gather one's thoughts **47** seine
Gedanken sammeln
threaded rod **164** Gewindestange
thriving **67** blühend, florierend
throughout **116** die ganze Zeit hindurch
to throw a curve ball **47** (mit einer Frage)
überrumpeln
ties **62** Verbindungen, Beziehungen
to tighten **94** straffen
time-consuming **17** zeitraubend
time limit **38** Zeitvorgabe, zeitlicher
Rahmen
time-bound **55** fristgebunden
time frame **115** zeitlicher Rahmen

lead time **15** Herstellungszeit
real time **67** Echtzeit
to play for time **93** Zeit gewinnen,
Zeit schinden
first-time **124** erstmalig, neu-
timeliness **55** Rechtzeitigkeit,
Pünktlichkeit
a number of times **102** mehrfach,
mehrmals
timescale **93** zeitlicher Rahmen
tolerance **86** Toleranz, Abweichung
ton **75** Tonne
on top **81** zusätzlich
kitchen top **88** Küchenarbeitsplatte
to touch on **65** kurz berühren, streifen
toward **106** in Richtung, gegenüber
wind turbine tower **10** Windkraftrad
town hall **13** Rathaus
old town **26** Altstadt
toy **130** Spielzeug
to track down **81** ausfindig machen, finden
to keep on the track **47** in der Spur bleiben
to keep track of sth **72** den Überblick
über etw behalten
trade link **12** Handelsverbindung
trade show **34** Handelsmesse
trade union **37** Gewerkschaft
trade-off **89** Kompromiss, Ausgleich
traffic **22** Verkehr, Zugriff
traffic jam **49** Verkehrsstau
traffic rate **23** Zugriffsquote
training provider **37** Anbieter von
Weiterbildungen
sales training **13** Verkaufstraining
transaction **36** Geschäft, Transaktion
to transfer **131** übertragen
to translate **102** übersetzen
public transport **38** öffentliche Verkehrs-
mittel
transportation **10** Transport
business traveler **80** Geschäftsreisende/r
to treat sb **51** jmdn behandeln
treatment **9** Behandlung

water treatment plant 9 Wasseraufbereitungsanlage, Kläranlage
to **trick** 69 täuschen, hereinlegen
to **trick sb into sth** 69 jmdn mit einem
Trick zu etw bringen
trillion 75 Billion
to **triple** 77 verdreifachen
Yours truly 157 Mit freundlichen Grüßen
trust 68 Stiftung
to **place trust in sb** 106 zu jmdm
Vertrauen haben, an jmdn glauben
truth 49 Wahrheit
truthful 106 ehrlich
try 10 Versuch
Have a try! 10 Versuch's mal!
to **try one's luck** 42 sein Glück versuchen
tube 94 Rohr, Röhre
tubing 10 Rohr, Schlauch
to **tune into sth** 59 sich auf etw einstellen,
sich in etw hineinhören/hineinversetzen
tunnel 116 Tunnel
turbine 10 Turbine
wind turbine tower 10 Windkraftrad
to **turn** 13 umdrehen
to **turn around** 40 wenden, umdrehen
to **turn up** 64 auftauchen, erscheinen
turn of phrase 73 Ausdrucksweise
in turn 112 wiederum
turn-taking 125 Sprecherwechsel
to **take it in turns** 38 sich abwechseln
24/7 48 24 Stunden, 7 Tage die Woche

U

ultraviolet 114 ultraviolett
unannounced 121 unangekündigt
unbiased 55 objektiv, unvoreingenommen
unchanged 163 unverändert
unclaimed 80 herrenlos, nicht abgeholt
to **undercut** 112 unterbieten
to **underestimate** 28 unterschätzen
underground 14 unterirdisch
undeveloped 117 nicht erschlossen
uneconomical 92 nicht wirtschaftlich

unfinished 107 unvollendet
unforeseen 129 unvorhergesehen, uner-
wartet
trade union 37 Gewerkschaft
business unit manager 15 Leiter/in des
Geschäftsbereichs
unlikely 115 unwahrscheinlich
unreadable 63 nicht lesbar, schwer zu lesen
to **unscramble** 110 entschlüsseln, entwirren
unsure 137 unsicher
unwilling 137 nicht bereit, widerwillig
to **unwind** 42 sich entspannen, abschalten
up and running 37 in Gang, funktionierend
up to a point 51 bis zu einem bestimmten
Punkt
to **uphold** 130 unterstützen, bestätigen
upscale 126 exklusiv, gehoben
urban 117 Stadt-, städtisch
usage 138 Verbrauch
usefulness 121 Nützlichkeit, Eignung
to **utilize** 66 verwenden, nutzen

V

vacancy 39 offene Stelle
valid 111 gültig
value management 127 Wertmanagement
to **take sth at face value** 111 etw für
bare Münze nehmen
vast 66 riesig
vendor 112 Verkäufer/in
venture 66 Unternehmung, Vorhaben
verify 92 überprüfen, bestätigen
versus 75 gegen, gegenüber
vertical 168 vertikal
viewpoint 137 Standpunkt, Blickwinkel
field visit 48 Vor-Ort-Termin,
Kundenbesuch
to **pay a visit** 50 einen Besuch abstatten
visual 69 Anschauungsmaterial
volume 38 Lautstärke, Volumen
vote 51 Abstimmung
VP (= vice-president) 6 Vizepräsident/in

W

to **waffle** *(coll.)* **47** schwafeln

to **walk up to sb** **64** auf jmdn zugehen

to **walk away from** **92** etw aus dem Weg gehen, vor etw davonlaufen

a **minute's walk** **26** ein Katzensprung

warranty **49** Garantie

flat **washer** **164** Unterlegscheibe

to **watch sth** **157** auf etw achten

water treatment plant **9** Wasseraufbereitungsanlage, Kläranlage

to **test the waters** **111** die Lage ausloten

wave **114** Welle

way *(coll.)* **53** viel

No way! **59** Auf keinen Fall!

to **get in the way of** **95** in die Quere kommen

way off **64** weit weg

well-known **41** bekannt

wet **43** nass

roulette wheel **42** Roulette

when in doubt **21** im Zweifel

whereas **76** während, dagegen

while **6** Weile

to **take a while** **6** eine Weile dauern

once in a while **95** von Zeit zu Zeit

to **whom it may concern** **157** an die zuständige Abteilung

widely **85** sehr, erheblich

to **widen** **41** erweitern

wildlife **117** Tierwelt

wind **10** Wind

wind turbine tower **10** Windkraftrad

win-win **89** gewinnbringend für beide Seiten

wisdom **69** Weisheit

conventional wisdom **69** herrschende Meinung

-wise **92** -mäßig, was ... betrifft

wishy-washy *(coll.)* **60** vage, wischiwaschi

to **withdraw** **111** zurückziehen, widerrufen

with reference to **22** mit Bezug auf, bezüglich

sequencing word **15** Gliederungswort

linking word **50** Verbindungswort

to **get a word in edgewise** **125** auch mal zu Wort kommen

wording **53** Formulierung

to **work sth out** **88** sich etw ausdenken

workflow **58** Arbeitsablauf

in working order **39** in betriebsfähigem Zustand

working knowledge **40** Grundkenntnisse

works of art **26** Kunstwerke

to **change for the worse** **78** sich zum Schlechteren verändern

worst case scenario **77** der schlimmste Fall, größter anzunehmender Unfall– GAU

to **wrap up sth** *(coll.)* **65** etw abschließen, beenden

technical writer **101** technische/r Redakteur/in

Y

Yours truly **157** Mit freundlichen Grüßen

Akron	['ækrɒn] 12
Arab Emirates	[ˌærəb 'emərəts] 80
Arabic	['ærəbɪk] 46
Bagsvaerd	['bəʊsvɛːɐ] 24
Bavaria	[bə'veəriə] ◉ 1.5
Belgium	['beldʒəm] 117
Benelux countries	['benɪlʌks kʌntriːz] 36
Budapest	[ˌbjuːdə'pest] 135
Bulgaria	[bʌl'geəriə] 102
China	['tʃaɪnə] 9
Darkhan	['dɑːkən] ◉ 2.02
Delhi	['deli] 124
Denmark	['denmɑːk] 8
Dutch	[dʌtʃ] ◉ 1.2
Eglington	['eglɪŋtən] ◉ 1.16
Finland	['fɪnlənd] 87
Finns	[fɪnz] ◉ 2.18
Florida	['flɔːrɪdə] 27
Hanseatic Hall	[ˌhænsiˌætɪk 'hɔːl] 1.10
Helsinki	[hel'sɪŋki] 9
Hungarian	[hʌŋ'geəriən] 28
Hungary	['hʌŋgəri] ◉ 1.7
India	['ɪndiə] 9
Kolding	['kəʊldɪŋ] ◉ 1.9

Milan	[mɪ'læn] 126
Møn	[møːn] ◉ 1.9
Mongolia	[mɒŋ'gəʊliə] 74
Päljänne	['pæijænɪə] ◉ 2.19
Pitkäkoski	['pitkækoski] ◉ 2.19
Poland	['pəʊlənd] 8
Poles	[pəʊlz] ◉ 2.18
Prague	[prɑːg] 37
Rhineland Palatinate	['raɪnlænd pəlætɪneɪt] 25
Romans	['rəʊmənz] 67
Rome	[rəʊm] 67
Seoul	[səʊl] ◉ 1.22
Singapore	[ˌsɪŋə'pɔː] ◉ 2.14
Slovakia	[sləʊ'vækiə] ◉ 1.28
Sofia	['səʊfiə] 102
Sonora	[sə'nɔːrə] 102
South Korea	[ˌsaʊθ kə'rɪə] ◉ 1.22
southern Germany	[ˌsʌðən 'dʒɜːməni] ◉ 1.5
Toledo	[tə'liːdəʊ] ◉ 1.11
Toronto	[tə'rɒntəʊ] ◉ 1.5
Ukraine	[ju'kreɪn] ◉ 1.28
Ulan Bator	[ˌjuːlən 'beɪtə] 75
Vanhakaupunki	['vanhakaupunki] ◉ 2.19

Irregular verb list

Infinitive	Simple past	Past participle	
be	was/were	been	sein
become	became	become	werden
begin	began	begun	beginnen, anfangen
break	broke	broken	brechen, kaputtmachen
bring	brought	brought	bringen
build	built	built	bauen
buy	bought	bought	kaufen
catch	caught	caught	fangen
choose	chose	chosen	(aus-)wählen, aussuchen
come	came	come	kommen
cost	cost	cost	kosten
cut	cut	cut	schneiden
deal	dealt	dealt	handeln, sich beschäftigen (mit)
do	did	done	tun, machen
draw	drew	drawn	zeichnen
drink	drank	drunk	trinken
drive	drove	driven	(Auto)fahren
eat	ate	eaten	essen
fall	fell	fallen	fallen
feel	felt	felt	(sich) fühlen
find	found	found	finden
fly	flew	flown	fliegen
forget	forgot	forgotten	vergessen
get	got	got (US: gotten)	bekommen, gelangen
give	gave	given	geben, schenken
go	went	gone	gehen, fahren
grow	grew	grown	wachsen
have	had	had	haben
hear	heard	heard	hören
hide	hid	hidden	(sich) verstecken
hit	hit	hit	schlagen
hold	held	held	halten
hurt	hurt	hurt	schaden
keep	kept	kept	behalten
know	knew	known	wissen, kennen
lead	lead	lead	führen, leiten
learn	learnt/learned	learnt/learned	lernen
leave	left	left	(weg)gehen, (ver)lassen

Infinitive	Simple past	Past participle	
lend	lent	lent	(aus)leihen, borgen
let	let	let	(zu)lassen, erlauben
lose	lost	lost	verlieren
make	made	made	machen, tun
mean	meant	meant	bedeuten
meet	met	met	(sich) treffen
pay	paid	paid	(be)zahlen
put	put	put	legen, stellen, setzen
read [ri:d]	read [red]	read [red]	lesen
ride	rode	ridden	(mit)fahren, reiten
rise	rose	risen	steigen, sich erheben
ring	rang	rung	klingeln, anrufen
run	ran	run	laufen, verwalten
say	said	said	sagen
see	saw	seen	sehen
sell	sold	sold	verkaufen
send	sent	sent	senden, schicken
set	set	set	setzen, stellen, legen
shake	shook	shaken	schütteln
show	showed	shown/showed	zeigen
sing	sang	sung	singen
sit	sat	sat	sitzen
sleep	slept	slept	schlafen
speak	spoke	spoken	sprechen
spell	spelt/spelled	spelt/spelled	buchstabieren, schreiben
spend	spent	spent	ausgeben, verbringen
spill	spilt/spilled	spilt/spilled	verschütten
stand	stood	stood	stehen
swim	swam	swum	schwimmen
take	took	taken	nehmen
teach	taught	taught	unterrichten
tell	told	told	erzählen, sagen
think	thought	thought	denken, meinen
throw	threw	thrown	werfen
understand	understood	understood	verstehen
wear	wore	worn	tragen, anhaben
win	won	won	gewinnen
write	wrote	written	schreiben

Notes